CONTENTS

PART I - COFFEE

PART II - TEA

THE COFFEE BOOK

FEATURING A SECTION ON TEAS

CHRISTIE KATONA
THOMAS KATONA

BRISTOL PUBLISHING ENTERPRISES, INC.
San Leandro, California

A Nitty Gritty® Cookbook

Printed in the United States of America.

ISBN 1-55867-051-3

Cover design: Frank Paredes
Front cover photography: John Benson
Food stylist: Suzanne Carriero
Illustrator: James Balkovek

THE HISTORY OF COFFEE

By most accounts the discovery of coffee took place around 600 A.D. It is widely believed that Ethiopian tribesmen discovered the coffee plant growing in the wild while tending their herds. The tribesmen mixed the ground berries with animal fat and rolled the resulting mixture into balls for eating during their journeys (perhaps their version of "No Doz" pills). For the next 400 years the berries were used primarily for food (although some resourceful person discovered the berries could be fermented into wine). The use and cultivation of the beans eventually migrated to Arabia, where somewhere between 10th and 15th centuries (the scholars are still arguing about when), the Arabs learned to steep the beans in water to make a delicious brew they called "qahwa." The brew, considered by some to be a potent medicine, was known for its restorative powers as well as being a delicious beverage. By the end of the 15th century Arabian coffee houses were popular meeting places and coffee was an established part of Arabian life.

As early as the 13th century, Arabia was shipping coffee from Arabian ports including Mocha, which is the source of the name for this famous coffee bean. The enterprising Arabian merchants who grew and sold the beans shrewdly prevented any viable seeds and coffee plants from being exported to protect their monopoly on the product. For several hundred years they successfully kept the source of the beans to themselves and enjoyed a brisk trade and high profits.

However, as we all know, it is hard to keep a good thing to yourself forever. In the 17th century it is reputed that a Moslem pilgrim successfully smuggled a plant and/or seeds home to his native India. From this humble start, the first coffee plantation in India was started at Karnatak and quickly spread to dozens of countries within a very short span of time. Dutch traders purchased some of the trees from the Karnatak plantation and began cultivating them in Java, which is the source of the Mocha Java blend.

A young French naval officer, Captain Gabriel Mathieu de Clieu, is credited with being responsible for bringing the plant to the Caribbean via Martinique, where it spread throughout the West Indies and eventually to Central and South America. The single plant he brought to Martinique appears to be the progenitor of most of the billions of coffee plants which are now the major source of the world's coffee. The plant acquired (stolen) by De Clieu was a descendent of a coffee plant given as a gift to Louis XIV. The king's coffee plants were cultivated in a hothouse at Louie XIV's Jardin des Plantes and were kept under close guard. De Clieu was able to obtain one of the plants through a romantic liaison with a lady of the court who had access to the hothouse; the rest is history.

Romance also played a part in the spread of coffee production to Brazil. There is evidence that Brazil clandestinely acquired the plant through Dutch Guianna, where a Brazilian Army Lieutenant smuggled the plant back to Brazil with the aid of the wife of the local governor who was enamored with the Lieutenant.

Coffee use spread from Arabia first to Turkey and eventually to Europe. It appears that Venetian traders were responsible for introducing coffee to European markets. The first coffee house in England opened in 1637 and within three decades had spread throughout the country. English coffeehouses became a center for social, intellectual, commercial and political discussions. These coffeehouses became known as "penny universities" because by paying a penny admission price, you could hear intellectual discussions as well as the latest gossip and news while enjoying your cup of coffee.

In the American colonies, the Dutch had introduced English style coffeehouses, but until the American revolution and the Boston Tea Party, tea was the preferred American beverage. Starting with the boycott of English tea, the beverage of choice in America became coffee and to date has remained the preferred beverage for most Americans.

COFFEE PRODUCTION

While there are many species of coffee trees in the world, only two have any economic significance, coffea arabica and coffea canephora, or as they are more commonly known, arabica and robusta coffees. Although both species originated in the same general region between Africa and Asia, they are now grown in numerous countries in a band stretching about 25 degrees north and south of the equator. The arabica beans are considered the higher quality "gourmet" beans while the robusta beans are less expensive and the primary bean used in the canned and instant coffee found in your local neighborhood grocery store.

The arabica coffee trees thrive at higher altitudes, generally between 5,000 and 8,000 feet. In these higher altitudes the beans mature at a slower pace, which gives them time to produce a richer, denser, more flavorful bean known in the trade as a "hard bean."

On the other hand, the robusta coffee trees grown in lower altitudes have many advantages for the producer. They are easier to cultivate, more disease-resistant, can tolerate larger temperature and moisture extremes, produce more beans, and their fruit matures considerably quicker than their arabica counterparts. They also have about twice as much caffeine which partly accounts for their harsher taste. The net result is a bean which is cheaper to produce albeit less flavorful.

The coffee tree is an evergreen which grows to about fifteen feet high and ten feet across; however, on farms and plantations the trees are typically trimmed to no more than eight or nine feet high and about six feet across to facilitate harvesting. Coffee trees start to produce blossoms at three to fours years of age and are fully mature at about seven years.

The coffee tree's blossoms are creamy white with a sweet-smelling fragrance resembling orange blossoms or jasmine. The blossoms eventually close and develop into small sweet berries somewhat like elongated cranberries which are at first green, then ripen into bright crimson fruit called *cherries*. The arabica tree cherries ripen in about six to nine months while robusta trees take only about three months to mature, mostly due to their lower growing elevation.

The coffee beans you grind at home are the seeds of these coffee cherries. Within the pulp of each cherry are two flat-sided seeds. Each seed has a thin, tight-fitting inner skin called the *silverskin* and a yellowish outer husk called the *parchment*. A healthy coffee tree produces about 2000 beans per year.

About one to three percent of a tree's cherries do not develop the second seed due to improper pollination. The remaining seed develops a rounded smaller bean known as a *peaberry* in the coffee trade. You might think these would be inferior, but peaberries are thought by a good part of the industry to be especially flavorful due to their unique development, and they are sold as a specialty item in coffee shops.

The coffee tree itself is somewhat unusual. Most fruit bearing trees first develop blossoms that mature together into fully ripened fruit. However, the coffee tree often has blossoms and both ripe and unripe cherries all at the same time and even on the same branch. This complicates the harvesting process and adds to the cost, especially at higher altitudes where the maturing process tends to be less even. The picker must return to the same coffee tree several times to pick only the ripe berries and to pick before the berries become overripe, which can be a matter of only a few days. Overripe berries are a dark red to purple and have a detrimental effect on the flavor of the coffee bean.

Most harvesting of quality beans is still done by hand; however, some countries like Brazil have been experimenting with mechanical harvesters which either shake the tree trunks or branches to retrieve the berries. The results of mechanical harvesting have not been good and the hand-picked method is still the method of choice for top quality coffee.

Coffee cherries are processed by either the wet or dry method. The dry method is the oldest and cheapest and is used primarily where water is in short supply or where wet processing equipment is not available. It consists of drying the fruit on the tree or shaking or stripping the fruit from the tree and then sun-drying it on cement or packed-earth patios. Generally this method results in inferior coffee because the underripe and overripe berries are processed along with the good beans. After the cherries are dried they are packed in bags and transported to mills in large cities where machines are used to remove the dried cherry pulp, the silverskin and the parchment. The beans are then sorted and graded according to the country's and local producer's methods.

The wet method consists of feeding freshly picked cherries through machines which separate the seeds from the pulp. As the mixture is fed through water, the lighter pulp floats to the top and is removed, leaving the seeds behind. The seeds are put into liquid-filled storage tanks for 24 to 48 hours and allowed to ferment slightly to remove an outer muscilage coating before final washing and drying.

After the fermentation process, the seeds are dried to about a ten percent moisture content. The drying is usually done on cement patios but more recently is done with tumbling dryers which greatly speed up the process. During the drying process the seeds shrink within their silverskin and parchment coverings. At this point, the dried covering and the beans themselves are referred to as *pergamino*. These pergamino beans can be stored for a considerable period without a significant effect on their flavor. The next stage of processing is to put the pergamino beans through hulling or milling machines which gently remove the silverskin and parchment coverings and give the beans a polished look. The longer the beans are milled, the more polished and attractive they appear. However, it is also possible to damage the beans if they are overmilled or exposed to too much heat. Heat produced from too much friction can remove the natural wax coating on the surface of each bean which seals in the volatile aromatic flavors. If over-processed, the complexity and quality of the final cup of coffee will be diminished.

The final stage before export is the sorting and grading of the beans. The sorting process is not consistent between coffee producing countries or even regions. Some countries sort primarily by size and shape, while other countries sort primarily by growth altitude. Higher altitude beans tend to be smaller and more dense and have both more veining on their sides and a narrower slot on the flat side. Experienced coffee buyers learn to observe and distinguish these physical characteristics but make their final assessment based on taste. Only about 20 percent of the graded beans are judged premium coffee beans.

CHOOSING COFFEE

WHERE TO BUY IT

While gourmet coffee was once the province of esoteric specialty shops, it is now available in large variety at most of the jumbo supermarkets. However, the specialty shops still have a much broader selection of coffee as well as coffee makers and accessories. We prefer the specialty shops just for the atmosphere, but you will also find they have both a broader knowledge of the product and a shared enthusiasm for the product that you just won't find in any supermarket. We still find it a wonderful experience to walk into a specialty store and find ourselves assaulted by an array of heady coffee aromas.

KNOWING YOUR BEANS

Although quality coffees are made from arabica beans, you may still be bewildered by the variety of arabica coffees available at your local coffee store. These stores offer a large selection of pure, unblended coffees usually distinguished by country of origin or perhaps by the major port from which they are exported. Coffee names such as Cinnamon, Full City, or French are used to distinguish coffees by the amount of roasting they have received.

Pure beans from each country and regions have unique flavor characteristics that are determined by their native climate and soil conditions. Retailers blend these pure coffees in an attempt to combine the best flavor characteristics of each country, and occasionally to offset a flavor characteristic which may be either too intense or dull by itself but makes a flavorful cup of coffee when blended with the right choice of beans from other countries. Many times the names of these blends have little to do with the source of the beans and are the product of retailers' creative imaginations. A quality store will usually post the type of beans used in the blend and provide samples to prospective customers. When in doubt let taste be your guide.

THE ROAST

In the roasting process the coffee finally yields its wonderful and subtle flavors. In principle it consists of heating green beans until they reach an internal temperature between 320° and 480°F. However, as most things in life, producing a quality roasted coffee is not that simple.

In most commercial operations, both radiant and convection heat is used to roast the beans within a rotating steel drum. This combination of the revolving drum and hot forced air is designed provide an even roast and also provides a method to collect the chaff that flakes off the beans during the process. After roasting, the beans are transferred into cooling bins where mechanical agitators keep the beans moving while either cool air is drawn through them (dry roast method) or fine water sprays (wet roast method) are used to cool them.

There are three roasting stages that the beans pass through as they progress from green beans to the rich brown coffee beans we find at the store. In the first stage, the roastmaster applies heat to bring the water in the beans close to the boiling point which drives off all free moisture in the beans: that is, all water that is not chemically bonded within the beans. In the second stage, heat, air flow and roasting time are carefully controlled by the roastmaster to bring the internal temperature of the beans to between 320° and 480°F (depending on the bean type and roast desired). During this stage, the cell walls of the coffee beans are broken down and the complex polysaccharides within are converted to starches and sugars. The natural sugars of the bean also caramelize, which results in the characteristically rich brown color of the roasted beans. This breakdown process, called pyrolosis, produces new substances not found in the original green bean. New aromatics substances are formed along with oils, fats, waxes and carbohydrates which add to the flavor complexity in the final brewed cup of coffee. The oils, fats, and carbohydrates provide body and help suspend and contain the many delicate and volatile aromatics within the cup.

As the roast continues, additional complex substances are broken down into simpler components and the many volatile oils are driven outward toward the bean's surface. This is considered the third stage and is characterized by an oily appearance on the outside of the bean. *Full city roast* is a term used to describe this approximate stage. It is the darkest roast achievable before the volatile oils are driven off by further application of heat. Going beyond this point such as for *French* or *Italian roasts* drives some of the aromatics completely from the beans (as well as some of the unique and distinguishing flavors). For these types of roasts, the roastmaster chooses to trade off those distinguishing varietal flavors in favor of the French roast taste that some people prefer. Luckily, the retail houses provide us with a tremendous variety of beans and roasts from which to choose.

The following terminology is in common use within the coffee industry. However, the terminology may vary somewhat by locale. For example French roast is a commonly used term for both the darker and darkest roast as shown below.

Light Roasts
Light
Pale
Cinnamon
Half City

Medium Roasts
Medium
Regular
Full City
American

Darker Roasts
Dark
Continental
Vienna or Viennese
New Orleans
French

Darkest Roasts
French
Italian
Espresso

TASTING

Ultimately, tasting is the most important method of judging coffee quality. Few of the millions of coffee drinkers within this country can accurately judge coffee quality or describe its characteristics except in the crudest of terms. However, industry coffee experts have developed a means of impartially evaluating coffee called *cupping* and a unique language for describing coffee's attributes.

To be a professional cupper, or coffee taster, requires years of experience and an extensive knowledge of coffee and coffee processing. However, a few basic terms should be in your repertoire. The three fundamental tasting terms you should be familiar with are flavor, body and acidity.

Flavor is the overall impression of aroma, body and acidity. It generally has two connotations. First, it can be used to describe taste in a general sense like "rich and mellow" or "bitter and harsh." Second, it can be used in a comparative sense, in which the brew might be described as tasting like nuts or a particular spice such as cinnamon, or for some less-than-perfect beans, like burnt rubber.

Body is the term used to describe the tactile impression of the weight and texture of the coffee within the mouth. Terms used to describe it range from "thin and watery" at one extreme to "buttery" and even "syrupy" at the other extreme. The sensation of oiliness within the mouth is a measure of the fat content, and the overall sensation of viscosity is a measure of the protein, carbohydrate and fiber content of the cup.

Acidity is a term used to describe how lively the cup is as opposed to being dull and flat tasting. It has nothing to do with how much acid it contains (pH factor). High acidity is one of the distinguishing characteristics of high grown arabicas and is considered a positive characteristic. Words used to further describe coffee acidity are those like crisp, sharp, keen, pungent or tangy. Another way to describe the acidity of a cup is in terms of how much "snap" it has. If a cup is described as having a lot of snap, it has a high acidity.

ESPRESSO

Most people associate the term *espresso* with a concentrated and bitter brew. But espresso done the proper way provides an extremely flavorful cup since it is brewed rapidly and served immediately while at its peak freshness. The term espresso is Italian for fast and primarily describes the method of preparation.

The espresso method uses pressure rather than gravity to rapidly extract the essence of the coffee in a concentrated form. Espresso is also used to describe the blend of beans and the degree of roast for the beans used to prepare espresso. Espresso roast is one of the darkest roasts and is characterized by a slightly burnt flavor.

Almost all coffee specialty shops now have professional espresso machines and serve both pure espresso and derivative espresso drinks to a growing number of enthusiasts. In the Seattle area, espresso has become something of a phenomenon. In addition to the specialty shops, curbside espresso carts and drive-through espresso windows have sprung up throughout the greater metropolitan area and it seems that every shopping mall and supermarket has its own espresso station.

If you want to prepare your own espresso there are many espresso machines available in specialty stores intended for home use. There are less expensive *Moka* pots which are heated on your burner to very sophisticated espresso machines. Prices run from just under $100 to about $700 depending on the features and quality desired. Gaggia, Krups, Pavoni, Bellina, Benjamin and Medwin, and Avanti are some of the better known brand names. The more sophisticated machines also have a cappuccino nozzle that uses the steam generated by the machine to steam and froth milk.

All of the machines work by forcing hot, pressurized water through finely ground espresso coffee that is tamped into a filter basket to make individual cups of espresso. Since pressure is used to extract the coffee essence, the variables of grind, quantity, tamp and rate of pour have a greater influence on the final taste than they do in the regular drip process for normal coffee.

You will have to experiment with the four variables since different brand machines have different operating pressures. Generally, the higher the operating pressure, the finer the grind of coffee you will use. Home machines generally operate in the area of 130 pounds per square inch (psi). The ideal water temperature is 193° to 197°F which may or may not be adjustable on your machine.

Beyond using good quality beans and fresh water, the secret to making good espresso is to avoid either under- or over-extracting the coffee essence. If the grind is too fine or the tamping too tight, the flow will be restricted, resulting in an over-extracted and bitter espresso. If the grind is too coarse or if the grinds are not tamped tightly enough, the water will flow too quickly, resulting in a thin and insipid espresso.

The right amount of espresso coffee is determined by the capacity of your machine. Generally, you will fill your filter insert almost completely, leaving just a little room for expansion of the grounds. Most home machines use about 1½ tablespoons per cup. The rate of pour is best determined by experiment. As a guideline your machine should produce about 1 to 1¼ ounces of espresso in about 25 seconds for a single shot machine.

You will find that there is an enormous variety of espresso-based drinks as well as flavored steamed milk drinks available at espresso bars. Below is a list of the basics you should find at any modern espresso stand:

Espresso Macchiato   An espresso "marked" with a dollop of milk foam.

Espresso con Panna   An espresso topped with a dollop of whipped cream.

Espresso Ristretto   A short pour (less than 1 ounce) which is accomplished by turning the pump off a few seconds earlier than normal.

Latte Macchiato   A cup of steamed milk "marked" with a spot of espresso. The steamed milk is added first, then topped with foam, and the espresso is added last by pouring it through the foam which leaves the "mark."

Caffé Latte   A shot of espresso added to steamed or foamed milk.

Caffé Mocha   Espresso mixed with steamed milk and chocolate syrup.

Cappuccino   This drink contains approximately ⅓ espresso, ⅓ hot steamed milk, and 1/3 foamed milk. Its name is derived from the foamy cap on the drink which resembles the white hooded robes worn by Capuchin friars.

Breve A latte made with steamed half and half milk.

Steamer Steamed milk with a flavored syrup. Almond, vanilla, and hazelnut are popular; however, there are flavors available that range from interesting to bizarre.

FLAVORED COFFEES

Many coffee purists are offended by the thought of adding any flavorings which would obscure the natural coffee flavors. However, flavored coffees have been around since the first coffee infusions were prepared in the Middle East. These early coffee drinkers included spices such as cinnamon, nutmeg, cardamom, pepper and nuts in their coffee.

Commercial flavored coffees are now made by spraying liquid or powdered flavorings over hot roasted beans and then quickly drying and packaging them. Coffee houses use both natural and artificial flavorings. Those houses which use only natural flavorings insist natural flavorings are better since they are more subtle and do not leave an artificial aftertaste in the mouth.

Flavored coffees generally have a more intense smell than taste due to the aromatic nature of the flavorings. Because aromatics have low boiling points by nature, their aromas are released continually along with the steam in the cup. The delicious smells imparted are savored as much as the taste by many consumers as witnessed by the fact that flavored coffees are now the fastest growing specialty market for coffee retailers.

The large supermarkets are cashing in on this trend and do a thriving business in flavored coffees. Some of the more popular flavored coffees are Irish creme, chocolate, vanilla, Swiss mocha, amaretto and macadamia nut.

Commercially flavored coffees first appeared in the early 1970s when there was a significant increase in coffee prices. The coffee purveyors found they could use lower grade beans (less expensive and less flavorful) which could be made salable by the addition of flavorings. Although the original reason for flavoring coffee was an economic one, the market response was strongly favorable, and as a result, flavored coffees are now a permanent item on the shelves of both specialty shops and supermarkets. Although some purveyors still use inferior beans, the better specialty stores insist on using only the highest quality beans, even for their flavored coffees.

DECAFFEINATED COFFEES

The stimulating affect of caffeine on the nervous system is well known and the increased alertness it provides is considered a desirable side benefit to many drinkers. However, the effects of caffeine are also a serious concern to many health-conscious people. Part of the reason for their concern is that there has been much misinformation in the press and in general literature about caffeine which has caused confusion among those consumers with health concerns.

Caffeine is a mild central nervous system stimulant that in moderate amounts poses no health problems to most individuals. But it is also known that excessive consumption can cause sleeplessness and irritate the stomach. The tolerance to caffeine varies so widely among individuals that you will have to be your own judge regarding the amount you can consume in a day without negative side affects. Some can drink many cups during the day, but find they must switch to decaf after 6 p.m. to get any sleep at night.

An average cup of caffeinated coffee contains 100 to 150 milligrams of caffeine, whereas, a cup of decaf contains 2 to 5 milligrams. If you have concerns about the amount of caffeine you are consuming, you can use these figures as guidelines but remember that actual caffeine content varies greatly depending on the coffee purchased and how it was prepared. Remember also that coffee may not be the only source of caffeine in your diet. Tea, chocolate, soft drinks like Coca-Cola, and some over-the-counter drugs like Excedrin and Dexatrim all contain varying amounts of caffeine.

There is also some concern about whether removing caffeine affects flavor and whether the process itself poses any health risk by leaving behind residual chemicals in the beans. Caffeine by itself is tasteless and odorless and its presence or absence has little or no affect on the flavor of the coffee. However, because all decaffeinating processes affect the chemical structure of the beans in varying degrees, they can and do affect the flavor in a negative way. The degree to which beans are affected depends on the process used. Generally, the processes can be grouped into either solvent-based or water-based although there are variations within each type.

The most commonly used solvent-based process, called the "direct contact" method, puts the solvent methylene chloride in direct contact with warmed coffee beans. Warming the beans first brings the caffeine closer to the surface for better extraction. Methylene chloride is very specific and dissolves the caffeine without affecting much else in the beans. Because of this, it is the preferred process for those trying to retain as much of the original flavor characteristics within the beans as possible. After the caffeine has been dissolved, the solvent is removed and the beans are dried. The solvent remaining in the green beans at this point is on the order of five parts per million. During subsequent roasting, the beans are subjected to temperatures of over 400°F where almost all traces of remaining solvent are driven off.

While methylene chloride seems like an ideal solvent for the processor, there is strong evidence that it is one of the substances contributing to the depletion of the ozone layer. For that reason, it is expected that it will be phased out of commercial use by 1995. Other solvents are available to take its place, but none is as specific as methylene chloride.

The most commonly used water-based process is called the *Swiss water process*. Its major advantage is that it uses only carbon-filtered water for processing. Its major disadvantages are that it is expensive and not very selective about what it removes from the beans. Besides the caffeine, it tends to remove many of the flavor-related oils and usually results in coffee with bland flavor characteristics.

You may have wondered why decaf beans are darker than regular caffeinated coffee. This is because the decaffeination process, whether solvent- or water-based, darkens the green beans. Because the beans are already dark, subsequent roasting makes them considerably darker than their caffeinated counterparts.

MAKING GOOD COFFEE

Regardless of the brewing equipment you choose to use, there are a few essentials to making good coffee at home:

1. Start with good quality beans.
2. Use clean equipment.
3. Use fresh water.
4. Use the correct grind for your equipment.
5. Use the right amount of coffee.
6. Use the right water temperature for brewing.
7. Serve coffee fresh.

The importance of good quality coffee beans is paramount. If you start with inferior beans, you can't expect to brew a great cup of coffee. Clean equipment is important as well. Remember that coffee contains oils and other substances that get deposited on your equipment. If not removed, these residual substances deteriorate when exposed to air and will taint subsequent batches of coffee. When cleaning those portions of the equipment that come in contact with the brew, avoid using dish soap since a small amount tends to remain and will add a flavor you did not want to your next pot. Instead, use a non-abrasive scrubber with a little baking soda and then rinse thoroughly with fresh water.

If you're lucky to have a clean, fresh-tasting water supply in your city, then cool running tap water will make a great cup of coffee. If your water has enough minerals or other substances to color the taste, then consider a water filter or bottled spring water. If using tap water, let the cold water run for a time to aerate the water. Remember that your final coffee is still about 98 percent water.

If coffee brewing is done properly, the brewed pot should contain between 18 to 22 percent of the ground coffee weight in extracted solubles. If it contains less, the coffee will taste bland and watery; if it contains a higher percentage, the brew will taste harsh and bitter. The amount of extraction is determined by the fineness of the coffee grind and the length of time that the hot water is in contact with the coffee grounds. As in making espresso, too fine or too coarse a grind will cause over- or under-extraction of the solubles. For automatic drip machines, which are the most common machines in home use today, the brewing cycle should take approximately four to six minutes for a drip grind. Finer grinds will be in the range of one to four minutes and the coarser grinds in the range of six to eight minutes. These of course are best approximations and may vary with the type of equipment you use.

The amount of coffee you should use for a full-bodied and flavorful cup of coffee is 2 level tablespoons per 6-ounce cup. People who try to skimp on the quantity of coffee or who grind coffee extra fine in an attempt to squeeze the maximum amount out of the grounds just end up with thin bitter coffee. If you go to all the trouble to buy quality beans and properly handle them to retain their flavor, don't ruin your coffee at this final stage of preparation by trying to stretch it.

Most experts believe the best brewing temperature for coffee is between 195°F and 205°F. This temperature provides the best extraction of the coffee essence from the beans. Automatic drip machines designed for home use have their thermostats set in this range but remember to use cold water to ensure consistency in the brewing time.

Finally, serve the coffee fresh. The flavorful aromatics in fresh brewed coffee start to evaporate immediately after brewing and there is a noticeable loss of flavor after about 20 minutes if left on the hot plate. Probably the best and easiest course of action is to pour the freshly brewed coffee into a vacuum thermos bottle where it will retain its freshness far longer than sitting out in the open.

COFFEE BREWERS

There are a wide variety of coffee brewers on the market. By far the most popular home units are the *automatic drip coffee makers* because of their ease of use and the fact that they are priced in a range most people can afford. They make a pretty good cup of coffee, especially since additional accessories like metal mesh filters have become widely available.

Espresso machines are fairly popular, but the higher cost and extra skill required to make a good cup have kept some buyers at bay. We think that as the number of espresso machine brands grows, competition for those consumers who haven't yet taken the plunge will force manufacturers to design machines in a price range more in line with what the general public is willing to pay. After that, espresso machines should be as popular as the automatic drip machines are today.

Percolators, with which the over-thirty crowd grew up, are still around but are not recommended for good coffee. They recirculate the brewed coffee from the bottom of the pot to the top to drench the coffee grounds over and over. This boiling of the coffee and over-extraction of the grounds tends to make the coffee bitter.

A *French press* is a type of plunger pot which produces a cup with a lot of body. After coffee grounds are added to the container, hot water is poured over them and the mixture is allowed to steep for a period. Then a plunger is used to force the grounds to the bottom of the container, leaving the brewed coffee above. Because a mesh screen is used instead of paper filters, the resulting coffee has more suspended oils and other substances to remain in the brew which some people prefer. This type of brewer is a little harder to clean up and since the grounds remain somewhat in contact with the liquid, the brew tends to take on a strong taste after awhile.

A *vacuum pot* is an unusual and interesting way to make coffee. It consists of an upper and lower glass pot which can be separated. The upper pot contain a filter assembly and a glass tube at the bottom. The glass tube extends from about the middle of the upper pot through its bottom into the lower pot. The bottom pot is filled with cold water, then the upper pot is inserted into the lower pot which seals tightly. Coffee grounds are placed in the upper pot over the filter assembly and then a heat source is applied to the lower pot. When the water boils it is forced up the glass tube into the upper pot where it steeps the coffee grounds. The heat source is then turned off. As the lower pot cools, the vacuum created draws the coffee in the upper pot through the filter. After the process is complete, the upper pot assembly is removed. This makes for a fascinating display which you may want to use at dinner parties as part of the entertainment.

There are a number of other interesting brewers you will find in your specialty store like *cold water extractors, Italian Neapolitan flips* and other stove-top units, and *Turkish ibriks,* all of which can make good coffee.

STORING COFFEE AT HOME

Coffee, by its nature, is such that its many complex flavors are just at their peak as they leave the roaster. Unfortunately, coffee's wonderful flavor and aroma also begin to deteriorate immediately after roasting if left exposed to air. Exposure to air causes the oils responsible for coffee's flavor and aroma to evaporate. Unless protected in some manner, whole beans have only about a two-week life before their freshness and peak flavors disappear. The flavor and aroma of ground coffee will deteriorate within hours since it has much more surface area exposed to the air.

The best advice is to keep whole beans in an airtight container until ready to use and then grind only the amount you need to use. If you need to store coffee beans for longer lengths of time (up to three months), the best method is to place the beans in airtight containers and freeze them. You may want to store the beans in several small containers in the freezer because returning thawed unused beans to the freezer will result in moisture condensation which also causes flavor loss.

COFFEE TRIVIA

- Coffee is a natural beverage with no added sugar or preservatives. The average cup of home-brewed coffee costs about 8 cents; the average cup of a soft drink at home costs approximately 20 cents.

- The faster the brewing method for your coffee, the finer the grind.

- Always use fresh, cold tap water for brewing. Hot water flattens the taste of coffee.

- Never reheat coffee: after 20 minutes it loses its peak flavor. If you must keep brewed coffee, store in a thermos or vacuum container.

- Coffee may be frozen for up to 3 months without losing quality.

- Arabica beans account for 90% of the world's coffee output.

- Robusta beans are twice as high in caffeine and acidity as Arabica.

- Arabica coffee beans, like fine wine, take flavor from the soil, climate and altitude in which they are grown.

- In 1683, William Penn paid $4.68 for a pound of coffee.

- The average American adult consumes 26.7 gallons of coffee per year.

- 450,000,000 cups of coffee are consumed per day in the United States.
- The top three coffee producing countries in the world today are Brazil, Colombia and Indonesia in that order.
- The value of coffee imported by the United States in 1990 was over 4 billion dollars.
- The average American adult consumes 10.2 pounds of coffee beans per year.
- The average Swedish adult consumes over 13.4 pounds of coffee beans per year.
- The United States consumes over 20% of the world's coffee.
- The amount of caffeine in a average cup of coffee is 100 milligrams.
- The amount of caffeine in an average cup of espresso is 80 milligrams.
- In 1732 Bach wrote a coffee cantata.
- In 1670 the first license to sell coffee in the Colonies was granted from the British government to a woman in Boston.
- Each coffee tree produces about 2,000 cherries per year.
- Tea contains half as much caffeine as coffee.

- The most popular beverages in the world are: water, tea and coffee, in that order.
- Green coffee beans keep indefinitely.
- Roasted coffee beans lose most of their flavor within 2 weeks if they are not specially packaged.
- In Turkey and Greece it is customary for the oldest person present always to be served his coffee first.
- Italians like their espresso with lemon.
- Austrians like their coffee with whipped cream.
- Belgians like their coffee with chocolate.
- Swiss and Germans like to combine equal parts of coffee and hot chocolate.
- The French like their traditional cafe au lait, or equal quantities of coffee and hot milk.
- The Mexicans like cinnamon with their coffee.
- In Africa and the Middle East it is customary to add spices such as cardamom to coffee.
- Moroccans add peppercorns and Ethiopians add a pinch of salt to their brew.

COFFEE DRINKS

THE EVER POPULAR LATTE

A good latte consists of a freshly drawn shot of espresso combined with steamed milk, heated to between 150° and 170°F and then topped by 1/4 inch of foamed milk. Many syrups and toppings can be added to the latte. We find that fruit flavors go better with cold coffee and are delightful in the summer when added to Italian sodas. Fruit syrups are very good added to steamed milk, when they are called a "steamer."

The most popular brands of syrups include Stasero, Torani and Davinci. Listed here are some of the flavors, and new ones are being added to the line up every week. The newest flavor in our neighborhood is Red Licorice, made by combining licorice and red raspberry syrups.

continued next page

LATTE FLAVORS

almond
amaretto
banana
blackberry
blueberry
boysenberry
cherry
chocolate
cinnamon
coconut
coffee
creme de cacao
creme de menthe
grand orange
grape

hazelnut
Irish cream
kiwi
lemon
licorice
lime
orange
orgeat
passion fruit
peach
raspberry
strawberry
tamarind
vanilla

TOPPINGS AND ADDITIONS

cinnamon
cocoa powder
honey

nutmeg
sugar
vanilla powder

COFFEE DRINKS

Here are some interesting variations of coffee drinks and ideas to get you started creating your own combinations.

- **What's the Use?** - a latte made with decaf coffee and skim milk
- **Mocha Lite** – a mocha latte made with sugar-free cocoa
- **Chocolatino** – a mocha latte made with Mexican chocolate
- **Mud Slide** – a double shot of espresso mixed with chocolate and topped with whipped cream
- **Mocha Moo** – a mocha latte with almond
- **Almond Moo** – a latte with almond syrup
- **Mt. Saint Helens** – three shots of espresso topped with whipped cream
- **Mocha Mint** – a mocha latte with mint syrup
- **White Cow** – a mocha latte with vanilla syrup
- **Banana Gorilla** – a mocha latte with banana syrup
- **Almond Joy** – a mocha latte with almond and coconut syrup

- **Mounds** — a mocha latte with coconut syrup
- **Milky Way** — a mocha latte with caramel ice cream topping stirred in
- **Egg Nog Latte** — a latte made with steamed egg nog
- **Mocha Nog** — a mocha latte made with steamed egg nog
- **Apple Pie** — a latte with apple and cinnamon syrup
- **Irish Cream Breve** — a latte made with Irish Cream syrup and half and half
- **Red Licorice** — a latte made with red raspberry and licorice syrups

AFTER-DINNER COFFEES

The combination of good after-dinner coffee with a touch of liqueur and topped with whipped cream is hard to beat. Besides the usual Irish coffee, try making one of these delicious combinations. If you wish a sweeter drink, add brown sugar to the coffee or sweeten the whipped cream.

BASIC RECIPE for one serving

6 oz. freshly brewed hot coffee　　　whipped cream
liqueur of your choice

Pour coffee into a cup, stir in liqueur and top with whipped cream.

MOCHA
　1 oz. Kahlua
　1 oz. creme de cacao

KAUAI NIGHTCAP
　1 oz. Tuaca
　1 oz. Grand Marnier

KOLOA COFFEE
　1 oz. brandy
　1 oz. macadamia nut liqueur

KONA NUT
　1 oz. Kahlua
　1 oz. Frangelico

BROWN VELVET

1 oz. Triple Sec
1 oz. creme de cacao

MINT PATTY

1 oz. creme de menthe
1 oz. cream de cacao

SPANISH EYES

1 oz. Kahlua
1 oz. rum

ALEXANDER

1 oz. creme de cacao
1 oz. brandy

ANGEL WINGS

1 oz. creme de menthe
1 oz. brandy

AMORE

1 oz. amaretto
1 oz. brandy

ROYALE

1 oz. cognac
1 oz. Grand Marnier

MEXICAN

1 oz. Kahlua
1 oz. tequila

IRISH EYES

1 oz. Irish whiskey
1 oz. Bailey's Irish Cream

IRISH NUT

1 oz. Bailey's Irish Cream
1 oz. Frangelico
1 oz. Irish whiskey

HOMEMADE COFFEE LIQUEUR

1 quart

Store this easy-to-make liqueur in a dark place to age for two weeks before serving.

2 cups sugar
2 cups water
2 oz. instant coffee granules
1½ cups brandy or vodka
1 vanilla bean, cut in half lengthwise

Bring sugar and water to a boil, stirring to dissolve sugar. Add coffee and simmer for 3 minutes. Cool. Add brandy and vanilla bean. Pour into a bottle, seal and store at room temperature for two weeks. Strain out vanilla bean before serving.

IRISH CREAM LIQUOR

Try this wonderful mixture in your next cup of after-dinner coffee.

1 cup Irish whiskey
4 eggs
1 tsp. vanilla extract
1 tbs. chocolate syrup
1 can (14 oz.) sweetened condensed milk
¼ tsp. coconut extract

Combine ingredients in a food processor or blender. Store in the refrigerator.

THAI ICED COFFEE

Tom was with the U.S. Air Force in Thailand during the Viet Nam war. For many years after he told me about the wonderful iced coffee, I would try recipe after recipe to no avail. Finally Thai food became very popular in Seattle, and we were able to get authentic Thai coffee and produce the genuine article at home. Imagine our surprise when we read the ingredient label and found coffee, corn and sesame among the ingredients — we are positively addicted to this wonderful drink and enjoy it with everything from Equal and skim milk to cream and sugar!

To make **Thai Iced Coffee**: Use a drip coffee maker and grind the coffee mixture to medium texture. Use 4 oz. ground Thai coffee for a 10-cup capacity coffee maker. Brew as usual. Serve the coffee over ice in a tall glass. Add cream and sugar to taste, or sweetened condensed milk. Store any remaining coffee in the refrigerator.

Thai coffee (the 16 oz. package is labeled: O-LEANG POIUOER) is available from Oriental markets or: BANGKOK MARKET, INC.
2849 Leonis Blvd.
Vernon, CA 90058

MOOSE MILK

This recipe comes from the wilds of Canada, hence the name.

1½ quarts milk
1 quart half and half
1 cup creme de cacao
1 cup Kahlua
1 fifth dark rum
½ gallon ice cream
nutmeg

In a large bowl, break the ice cream into chunks. Pour other ingredients over the top and stir. Ladle into cups and dust with nutmeg.

APPETIZERS AND MAIN DISHES

PORK SATAY

Thai in origin, this makes a fun appetizer for a summer evening. Satay are also good with chicken or beef.

2 lb. pork tenderloin
2 garlic cloves, minced
1 tbs. salad oil
2 tsp. chili powder
2 tsp. coriander

1 tsp. ginger
3 tbs. brown sugar
1 tbs. lemon juice
1/4 cup coffee

Slice pork 1/4 inch thick and 1 inch wide. Combine all ingredients in a glass dish and marinate pork several hours or overnight.

To prepare, remove pork from marinade and blot dry with paper towels. Thread on bamboo skewers. Broil or grill over hot coals until pork is cooked through, about 4 minutes on each side. Serve with *Peanut Sauce*, page 45, or plum sauce.

PEANUT SAUCE

This sauce is very complex in flavors and you can adjust the "heat" to suit your taste. It freezes well and is always a hit.

1 tbs. oil
1 onion, chopped
2 garlic cloves, minced
1 cup chunky peanut butter
1 cup coconut milk
½ cup milk
2 tbs. fish sauce or soy sauce
3 tbs. brown sugar

1 tbs. lemon juice
1 tbs. lime juice
3 bay leaves
¼ tsp. cinnamon
1 tsp. curry powder
½ to 1 tsp. chili paste or cayenne pepper, to taste

Heat oil in a large saucepan and sauté onion and garlic until soft. Add remaining ingredients and stir with a whisk until blended. Simmer 5 minutes. Taste and adjust seasonings to your personal preference. Cool and remove bay leaves. Store in the refrigerator or freeze. This sauce goes well with chicken or beef satay.

PICADILLO

This makes a delicious appetizer served with tortilla chips. Or serve it over rice as a main course; pass sour cream, salsa, guacamole, shredded cheddar and sliced green onions to go on top.

1 cup raisins
1 cup hot coffee
2 lb. lean ground beef
2 onions, finely chopped
2 garlic cloves, minced
1 tbs. olive oil
2 tart apples, peeled, cored and
  coarsely chopped

1 cup chopped pimiento-stuffed
  green olives
1 can (14 oz.) stewed tomatoes
1 can (4 oz.) diced green chiles
salt and pepper to taste
½ tsp. cinnamon
½ tsp. cloves
1 cup slivered almonds, lightly toasted

Pour hot coffee over raisins and set aside to plump. In a large skillet, heat olive oil and sauté meat, onions and garlic until cooked. Drain off any excess liquid. Drain coffee from raisins; add raisins to meat mixture along with remaining ingredients, except almonds. Cook over medium heat for 10 minutes, stirring occasionally. Taste and correct seasoning. Stir in almonds and serve.

BEV'S BEST POT ROAST

Servings: 6 to 8

This unusual recipe for pot roast is similar to a variation of German sauerbraten. The vinegar tenderizes the meat overnight and adds flavor, while the coffee makes a rich base for gravy.

1 (4 to 5 lb.) chuck roast
4 garlic cloves
1 onion, sliced
1 cup raspberry vinegar

2 tbs. salad oil
2 cups brewed coffee
3 cups water

The day before serving, cut slits into meat and insert cloves of garlic into cuts. Place roast in a shallow bowl and top with onion slices. Pour vinegar over meat, cover and refrigerate overnight; turn occasionally.

The next day, remove meat from marinade and pat dry. Discard vinegar-onion mixture. Heat oil in a large roaster. Brown beef on both sides over medium high heat. Add coffee. Bake at 325° for 2 to 4 hours, or until meat is fork-tender.

If desired, add potatoes, carrots and onions around roast the last 45 minutes of cooking.

LAMB IN PITA

Servings: 8

A nice casual supper. You can prepare the meat mixture and sauce the night before.

2 lbs. lamb, cubed
1 tbs. oil
2 onions, chopped
2 carrots, chopped
1 garlic clove, minced
1 can (16 oz.) tomatoes, well drained
½ cup dark raisins
1 tbs. chili powder

1 tsp. curry powder
1 tsp. salt
1 tsp. sugar
½ tsp. cloves
½ tsp. cinnamon
½ cup coffee
salt and pepper to taste

In a large skillet, brown lamb in oil until brown. Add onion, carrots and garlic and cook until soft. Add remaining ingredients and cover. Simmer until tender, about 1 to 1½ hours. Split pita bread and fill with meat mixture. Serve with yogurt sauce.

YOGURT SAUCE

8 oz. unflavored yogurt
½ cucumber, seeded and diced

½ onion, chopped
2 tsp. dill

Combine ingredients and chill.

GUT-BUSTER CHILI

The flavor of this zesty chili is even better if it is made the day before serving. Serve with shredded cheddar cheese, diced onion, cilantro and sour cream for topping.

4 lb. coarsely ground beef for chili
2 yellow onions, chopped
2 garlic cloves, minced
2 green peppers, cored, seeded
  and chopped
1 can (14 oz.) diced canned tomatoes
1 can (8 oz.) tomato paste
1 can (8 oz.) diced green chilies

2 cups brewed coffee
¼ cup chili powder
3 tbs. cocoa powder
1½ tbs. cumin
½ tsp. crushed red pepper
2 tsp. salt, or to taste
2 bay leaves
finely grated zest of one orange

In a large soup kettle, sauté beef, onion and garlic. Drain off excess liquid. Add remaining ingredients and simmer for 1 hour until flavors are developed and mellowed.

HOLIDAY CHICKEN

This recipe is also good with Cornish game hens.

4 whole chicken breasts, with bones
   and skin
¾ cup strong coffee
½ cup brandy
¼ cup salad oil
¼ cup honey

juice and zest of 1 lemon
¾ cup prepared mincemeat
1 tbs. cornstarch
2 tbs. water
parsley and orange slices for garnish

The day before you plan to serve this dish, divide chicken breasts in half and place in a shallow ovenproof casserole. Combine coffee, brandy, oil, honey, lemon juice and zest. Pour over chicken, cover and refrigerate overnight.

Preheat oven to 375°. Pour off ¾ cup of the marinade. Bake chicken, uncovered, skin side down, for 20 minutes. Turn skin side up and continue cooking for 10 to 20 minutes longer, until chicken is done. Test by making a small cut with a knife in the thickest part of one piece.

Place ¾ cup of the marinade in a small saucepan. Combine cornstarch and water; add to marinade. Bring to a boil over medium heat and stir in mincemeat. Whisk until heated through. Remove chicken to a large platter, pour sauce over and garnish with parsley and orange slices.

BARBECUED BEEF

Serve this spicy beef on toasted sourdough rolls. A big green salad makes a great accompaniment.

1 (3 to 4 lb.) eye-of-the-round roast

MARINADE
2 tbs. instant coffee
1/2 cup water
1/3 cup cider vinegar
1/4 cup salad oil
1 cup catsup
1 tsp. salt

1/2 tsp. pepper
1 tsp. chili powder
1 tsp. celery seed
2 garlic cloves, minced
4 drops Tabasco, or to taste

Combine marinade ingredients. Place trimmed beef in a large plastic bag and pour marinade over. Refrigerate overnight, turning occasionally. Remove beef from marinade and grill over medium coals for 45 to 60 minutes or until meat tests rare with a meat thermometer, 140° when measured in the thickest part. To serve, thinly slice beef and serve on toasted rolls. May be served hot or cold. Spicy mustard and thinly sliced onions and dill pickles are good with this.

CHICKEN PAPRIKA

Servings: 8

The coffee adds a depth and richness to this recipe.

4 whole chicken breasts, halved
1 tsp. salt
1 tbs. paprika
½ cup butter
1 large onion, chopped
2 tbs. flour

1 tbs. paprika
1 cup coffee
3 tbs. tomato paste
¼ cup sherry
1 cup sour cream

In a plastic bag, combine salt and paprika. Shake chicken until evenly coated. In a large skillet, brown chicken in melted butter. Remove chicken and place in an ovenproof casserole. In the drippings, sauté onion until soft. Blend in flour and paprika to form a paste. Add coffee and tomato paste and stir until blended. Add sherry and sour cream. Pour sauce over chicken. Cover tightly and bake at 350° for 1 hour. Serve with noodles.

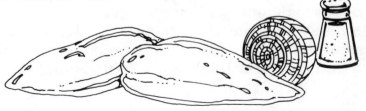

MAHOGANY RIBS

Servings: 4 to 8

Parboiling the ribs in water, garlic and a dash of cider vinegar tenderizes them and adds flavor while decreasing the cooking time.

4 lb. country-style spareribs
1 cup coffee
½ cup molasses
2 cloves garlic, minced
¼ cup Dijon mustard
3 tsp. Worcestershire sauce
½ cup cider vinegar
1 tsp. chili powder

Place ribs in a large pot and cover with cold water. Add ¼ cup cider vinegar and 1 tsp. garlic salt or powder. Bring to a boil, turn heat to low and simmer for 15 minutes. Drain well.

In a small saucepan, combine coffee with remaining ingredients. Simmer over low heat until blended. Place ribs in a shallow ovenproof casserole. Pour sauce over. Cover and bake at 325° for 1¼ hours or until tender.

COUNTRY HAM WITH RED EYE GRAVY

Servings: 4

In the true Southern tradition, this country ham is served with grits. The grits recipe is from Tom's mother and we all love it. If you're not fond of hot food, use plain cheese instead of the jalapeño.

4 ¼-inch slices country ham
1 cup water

2 tbs. black coffee

Cook ham slices in a heavy skillet over low heat until lightly browned, about 15 minutes. Remove and keep warm. Stir water and coffee into skillet. Bring to a boil and scrape up any brown bits from skillet. Serve gravy over ham and grits.

MARY'S GREAT GRITS

Servings: 6

4 cups water
dash of salt
1 cup grits
½ cup butter

2 eggs, beaten
1 tube Kraft Jalapeño Cheese Spread
   (or about 1 cup of shredded cheddar)
1 tsp. seasoning salt

Bring water to a boil in a saucepan. Add grits and stir to combine. Cook for 5 minutes over medium low heat. Add remaining ingredients and pour into a buttered casserole. Bake at 350° for 30 to 40 minutes.

GUSSIED UP BAKED BEANS

Servings: 8

These go great with a family barbecue of burgers and hot dogs.

½ lb. bacon, diced
1 large yellow onion, chopped
2 cans (16 oz. each) baked beans
½ cup molasses
½ cup brewed coffee
½ cup brown sugar
¼ cup catsup
1 tbs. mustard

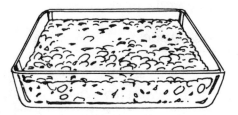

Sauté bacon and onion until bacon is beginning to crisp and onion is limp. Drain off any excess fat. Combine with remaining ingredients in a large ovenproof casserole. Bake at 350° for 30 minutes, or until bubbly.

CITRUS GRILLED RIBS

Servings: 6

Prepare the sauce in advance to allow the flavors to mellow. It's great on burgers, chicken or spareribs on the grill.

6 lbs. country-style pork ribs
3 tbs. oil
1/3 cup hoisin sauce
1/3 cup soy sauce
1 tbs. grated fresh ginger

3/4 cup whiskey
1/4 cup orange juice
1/4 cup grapefruit juice
1/4 cup brown sugar
2 tsp. fresh garlic, minced

Parboil ribs in water to cover adding a dash of cider vinegar and a tsp. of garlic salt. Simmer for 20 minutes and drain. Combine remaining ingredients and marinate ribs for 1 to 2 days in the refrigerator, turning occasionally. Drain ribs and discard marinade. Barbecue and baste with *Coffee Barbecue Sauce.*

COFFEE BARBECUE SAUCE

3 cups

1 cup double strength coffee
1 1/2 cups catsup
1/2 cup Worcestershire sauce
1/2 cup dark brown sugar

1/3 cup cider vinegar
1 tsp. crushed garlic
1 tsp. chili powder

Combine all ingredients in a large saucepan and simmer for 5 minutes. Cool and refrigerate.

CAKES, TORTES, CHEESECAKES, PIES AND CREPES

JAMAICAN RUM CAKE

Servings: 12 to 18

Extremely rich, this wonderful dessert is only for the most dedicated dessert lovers! Rich rum cake is topped with coffee butter cream, spread with Chocolate Satin and sprinkled with toasted almonds. The combination of flavors and textures is truly outstanding. This cake can be frozen.

RUM CAKE

½ cup butter
1 cup sugar
2 eggs
½ cup buttermilk
1 tsp. vanilla

1½ cups flour
1 tsp. baking powder
½ tsp. baking soda
½ tsp. salt

Preheat oven to 350°. With an electric mixer, cream butter and sugar until light. Add eggs, buttermilk and vanilla. Sift together flour, baking powder, soda and salt. Add to egg mixture and combine. Pour batter into a greased and floured 9x13-inch baking pan. Bake for 35 to 40 minutes or until cake tests done. While hot, poke holes in top of cake with a fork and pour *Rum Glaze* over the top.

RUM GLAZE

1 cup sugar
1/4 cup water
1/2 cup butter

3 tbs. dark rum - Meyers or Bacardi
  are good
1 tbs. vanilla

Heat combine sugar and water in a saucepan and bring to a boil. Add butter and stir until melted. Add rum and vanilla and pour over cake while hot. Let cake cool completely and spread with *Coffee Buttercream.*

COFFEE BUTTERCREAM

4 oz. white chocolate, melted
1/2 cup butter
1/4 cup powdered sugar

2 eggs
1 tbs. instant coffee
1 tsp. hot water

Using the steel knife of a food processor or an electric mixer, combine butter, melted white chocolate and powdered sugar until smooth. Dissolve coffee in hot water. Add to butter mixture along with eggs. Process until smooth. Spread on cooled cake. Refrigerate.

Spread top of cake with *Chocolate Satin*, page 84. Use as much or as little of the topping as you desire and freeze the remainder to frost brownies or other desserts. Sprinkle top of cake with 1 cup toasted slivered almonds. Store cake in the refrigerator. Let warm slightly before serving. Cut into small squares.

MOCHA CREME ROULAGE

Servings: 6 to 8

This dessert is like eating a cloud!

5 eggs, separated
1 cup sugar
3 tbs. water
6 oz. German sweet chocolate

1 cup heavy cream
1 tbs. instant coffee
¼ cup powdered sugar
1 tbs. powdered cocoa

Beat egg yolks with ¾ cup of sugar until thick and lemon colored. Melt chocolate with water. Cool. Stir chocolate into yolks. In a separate bowl, beat egg whites with an electric mixer, gradually adding remaining ¼ cup sugar. Fold whites gently into egg and chocolate mixture. Preheat oven to 300°. Butter a 11x15-inch jelly roll pan and line with parchment. Butter parchment. Spread batter evenly in pan. Bake at 300° for 15 minutes, turn oven to 350° and bake for 10 minutes.

Remove from oven and cover with a damp dish towel. Chill thoroughly. Remove towel and sprinkle heavily with cocoa. Turn over onto another sheet of parchment. Remove top piece of parchment. Whip cream with instant coffee and powdered sugar. Spread on top of roulage. Roll up like a jelly roll, using the bottom paper as a guide. Chill. Cut into slices to serve.

SPICE CAKE

Moist and flavorful, this cake keeps well. Mace is the outer covering of the nutmeg.

1 pkg. yellow cake mix
1 pkg. (3¾ oz.) instant butterscotch
  pudding
4 eggs
½ cup vegetable oil
1 cup brewed coffee

1 cup raisins
1 cup chopped pecans
1 tsp. cinnamon
1 tsp. nutmeg
½ tsp. allspice

Preheat oven to 350°. Combine all ingredients except nuts and raisins and beat with an electric mixer for 5 minutes. Add nuts and raisins. Pour into a greased and floured bundt pan. Bake for 45 to 50 minutes or until cake tests done. Cool 15 minutes; turn out onto a wire rack and cool completely.

CREAM CHEESE ICING

1 pkg. (8 oz.) cream cheese
2 cups powdered sugar
¼ cup butter

1 tsp. vanilla
brewed coffee to thin

Using the steel blade of a food processor, combine cream cheese, butter, powdered sugar and vanilla. Add coffee to thin to spreading consistency. Frost cake.

JAVA POUND CAKE

1 cake

This delicious coffee-flavored cake freezes well.

1 cup butter
1¼ cups sugar
4 eggs
½ cup brewed coffee
2¼ cups flour
1 tsp. baking powder
½ tsp. salt
2 tsp. vanilla
½ tsp. mace

Preheat oven to 325°. Using an electric mixer, cream butter and sugar until light and fluffy. Add eggs, beating well after each addition. Add coffee and vanilla. Sift dry ingredients together and add to creamed mixture. Pour into a well greased 9x5-inch bread pan which has been lined with parchment paper on the bottom. Bake for 1 hour and 25 minutes or until cake tests done. Cool in pan for 15 minutes and then turn out on a rack to cool completely.

COFFEE PECAN CHEESECAKE

Servings: 8 to 12

You'll love the combination of flavors in this rich, light-textured cheesecake.

CRUST

1 cup finely ground pecans
¼ cup sugar

2 tbs. butter

Combine ingredients and press into the bottom of a 9 inch springform pan. Bake at 350° for 10 minutes. Cool.

FILLING

1 pkg. unflavored gelatin
3 tbs. Meyer's dark rum
1 tbs. instant coffee
3 tbs. hot water

11 oz. cream cheese, softened
1 cup powdered sugar
1 cup whipping cream
2 tsp. vanilla

In a small saucepan, soften gelatin in rum. Place over low heat and dissolve. Cool slightly. Using the steel blade of a food processor, mix cream cheese with powdered sugar and vanilla. Dissolve coffee in hot water and add to cream cheese mixture. Add softened gelatin and blend. In a separate bowl, whip cream until soft peaks form. Combine cream cheese mixture with whipped cream. Pour into prepared crust. Chill. Garnish with whipped cream and pecan halves.

CAPPUCCINO CHEESECAKE

Servings: 8 to 12

My sister-in-law, Joanna, and I have been cooking together for years, both professionally and personally. She is a firm believer in the mixer, while I prefer the Cuisinart. In a side-by-side test making cheesecakes one day, we made one in the mixer and the other in the food processor. The texture and creaminess of the food processor cheesecake won hands down.

CHOCOLATE CRUMB CRUST

1 tbs. butter
1 pkg. (9 oz.) dark chocolate wafer cookies, finely ground
pinch of cinnamon
⅓ cup melted butter

Coat bottom and sides of a 9-inch springform pan with 1 tbs. butter. In a food processor using the steel blade, combine cookie crumbs, cinnamon and melted butter. Press crumb mixture evenly on sides and bottom of prepared pan. Bake at 325° for 5 minutes. Cool.

FILLING

1¼ lb. cream cheese, cut into 1-inch cubes
1¼ cups sugar
4 eggs, beaten
¾ cup whipping cream
¾ cup sour cream
¼ cup espresso coffee
1 oz. finely chopped semisweet chocolate
3 tbs. Kahlua
1 tsp. vanilla

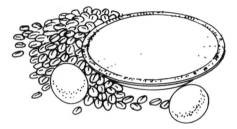

Using the steel blade of a food processor, combine cream cheese, sugar and eggs until smooth. Scrape sides down and add whipping cream and sour cream. Process to combine. Melt chocolate with espresso in the microwave and cool. Add chocolate mixture and liqueur to cream cheese mixture. Pour into prepared crust. Bake at 325° for 1 hour and 15 minutes, or until sides of the cake are set 2 inches in from the edges and center of cake is still puddinglike. Remove cake from oven and let cool on a wire rack until room temperature. Refrigerate cake overnight.

MOCHA CHOCOLATE CHIP CHEESECAKE

Servings: 12

For best results, always refrigerate a cheesecake overnight before serving.

CRUST
6 tbs. butter, melted
1½ cups chocolate wafer crumbs
2 tbs. sugar

Combine crust ingredients and press onto bottom and partially up sides of a buttered 10-inch springform pan. Bake at 350° for 10 minutes. Cool while making filling. Turn oven temperature to 200°.

FILLING

1½ lb. cream cheese, room temperature
1 cup sugar
4 eggs, room temperature
⅓ cup heavy cream
1 tbs. instant coffee powder
1 tsp. vanilla
6 oz. mini semisweet chocolate chips

Using the steel knife of a food processor, combine the cream cheese and sugar until light. Add the eggs and process until smooth, scrape down the sides of the bowl. Add the instant coffee and vanilla and combine.

Pour half of the filling into the prepared crust. Stir the chocolate chips into the remaining filling and carefully pour over the filling in the pan. Bake for 2 hours until set. Cool at room temperature. Cover with plastic wrap and refrigerate overnight.

PEANUT BUTTER TORTE

Servings: 8 to 12

A fantastic dessert to serve with coffee. The addition of molasses gives the peanut butter more depth. Jif is our favorite brand.

CRUST

1 cup graham cracker crumbs
1 cup chocolate wafer crumbs
¼ cup sugar

¼ cup melted butter
¼ cup peanut butter

Mix ingredients together and press in the bottom of a springform pan.

FILLING

8 oz. cream cheese
1 cup sugar
1 cup creamy peanut butter

1 tbs. molasses
1 tbs. vanilla
1 cup heavy cream, whipped

Beat cream cheese with sugar until light and fluffy. Add peanut butter, molasses and vanilla. Fold in whipped cream. Pour into prepared crust and smooth top. Cover and chill.

TOPPING

4 oz. semisweet chocolate, melted
2 tbs. butter
2 tbs. oil
½ cup chopped salted peanuts

Melt chocolate with butter and oil, stirring to combine. Cool slightly and spread on top of torte. Sprinkle with chopped peanuts and refrigerate. To serve, cut into wedges with a hot knife.

CHOCOLATE CHERRY TRUFFLE TORTE

Servings: 12 to 16

If you like chocolate-covered cherries, this one's for you!

2 jars (10 oz. each) maraschino
  cherries, drain and reserve ½ cup juice
2 cups butter
12 oz. semisweet chocolate

4 oz. unsweetened chocolate
1 cup sugar
8 eggs

Preheat oven to 325°. Line a 10-inch pan with parchment paper. Butter paper. Drain cherries and reserve ½ cup juice. Set aside 16 cherries to decorate top of cake. Using the steel blade of a food processor, coarsely chop cherries. Remove and set aside. Chop chocolates.

In a heavy saucepan, melt chocolate and butter. Pour melted mixture into the workbowl of the food processor and add sugar and cherry juice. Process until very smooth. Add the eggs one at a time. Stir in the chopped cherries. Pour into the prepared pan and bake in a water bath (bain marie) for 1 hour. Remove and cool on a wire rack. Frost and decorate with the cherries.

GANACHE FROSTING

2/3 cup heavy cream
2 tbs. butter
8 oz. semisweet chocolate

Heat cream in a small saucepan over medium heat. Stir in chocolate and butter to melt. Pour into a bowl and refrigerate for 1 hour, stirring occasionally, until thick and pudding-like. Frost torte and decorate with reserved cherries.

TOFFEE ICE CREAM TORTE

Servings: 8 to 12

Quick, easy and delicious. Be sure to pass extra sauce at the table.

1 cup almond macaroon crumbs
2 tbs. melted butter
1 quart chocolate ice cream, slightly softened
1 cup fudge sauce
1 quart coffee ice cream, slightly softened
4 Heath toffee bars, coarsely chopped

Combine crumbs and butter and press on bottom of a 9-inch springform pan. Bake at 350° for 8 to 10 minutes or until golden. Cool. Spread chocolate ice cream evenly on crust, drizzle with chocolate sauce and freeze until firm. Spread with coffee ice cream and sprinkle with chopped toffee. Drizzle with remaining fudge sauce. Cover and freeze until firm.

To serve, remove from freezer several minutes before slicing. Cut into wedges with a hot, wet knife.

ICE CREAM MERINGUE TORTE

Servings: 8

Often walnuts that are sold in packages at the grocery store have rubbed together and much of their skin comes off. When using walnuts in baking, you will get a much nicer result if you take the time to place the walnuts in a strainer and rinse them thoroughly with warm water. Shake to remove excess water and toast them briefly at 300° for 5 minutes; then proceed with your recipe.

3 egg whites, room temperature
1 cup sugar
22 Ritz crackers, crushed
½ tsp. baking powder

¾ cup chopped walnuts
1 tsp. vanilla
coffee ice cream
chocolate sauce

Using an electric mixer, beat egg whites until foamy. Add sugar gradually, beating until stiff. Fold in crackers, baking powder, nuts and vanilla. Butter a 9-inch pie pan.

Preheat oven to 325°. Pour mixture into prepared pan and bake for 30 minutes. Cool. To serve, cut into wedges and place a scoop of ice cream in the center. Top with chocolate sauce.

CASSATA

This rich Sicilian dessert uses purchased pound cake to speed preparation.

1 purchased pound cake
1 lb. ricotta cheese
2 tbs. whipping cream
¼ cup sugar
2 tbs. Grand Marnier

½ cup chopped candied fruit, such
  as cherries and orange peel
2 tbs. finely chopped toasted
  almonds, hazelnuts or pistachio nuts
2 oz. chopped semisweet chocolate

Trim ends off cake and slice it horizontally into fourths. In food processor or mixer, combine ricotta, cream, sugar, liqueur, fruit, nuts and chocolate. Place bottom layer of cake on a serving platter and spread with ⅓ of the cheese mixture. Repeat layers of cake and cheese, ending with cake. Refrigerate until firm, about 2 hours. Frost tops and sides. Decorate with remaining frosting. Cover and refrigerate 24 hours before serving for flavors to mellow. Slice to serve.

FROSTING

12 oz. semisweet chocolate
½ cup strong brewed coffee

1 cup butter

Melt chocolate with coffee. Beat with an electric mixer, adding butter a piece at a time. Chill to spreading consistency.

KAUAI PIE

Hawaii's version of the mainland's Mud Pie.

COCONUT CRUST

1½ cups butter cookie crumbs
½ cup flaked coconut

¼ cup melted butter
1 tsp. vanilla

Mix crust ingredients together and press into a 9-inch pie pan. Bake at 375° for 10 minutes and cool.

FILLING

½ gallon coffee ice cream
1 cup fudge sauce

2 cups macadamia nuts
½ cup flaked coconut

Soften ice cream slightly. Rinse macadamias if you wish to rid them of excess salt. Toast briefly at 375° for 5 minutes. Chop coarsely. Spread half of the ice cream in the bottom of the prepared crust, drizzle with half of the fudge sauce, half of the nuts and coconut. Repeat. Wrap and freeze until serving. To serve, thaw at room temperature for 10 to 15 minutes and cut into wedges.

KONA BANANA CREAM PIE

Whenever you make a graham cracker pie crust, add a teaspoon of vanilla — it improves the flavor immensely!

MACADAMIA NUT CRUST
1/4 cup macadamia nuts
1 cup graham cracker crumbs
1/4 cup sugar

1/4 cup butter, melted
1 tsp. vanilla

Using the steel knife of a food processor, combine crust ingredients. Press into a 9-inch pie plate. Bake at 375° for 10 minutes. Cool.

FILLING
3/4 cup sugar
5 tbs. flour
1/4 tsp. salt
1 cup coffee

1 cup evaporated milk
1 egg beaten with 1 tsp. milk
1 tsp. vanilla
3 bananas

In a heavy-bottomed saucepan, stir together sugar, flour and salt. Add coffee and evaporated milk. Bring to a gentle boil, whisking frequently until mixture begins to thicken. In a small bowl, beat egg, milk and vanilla. Add ¼ cup of the hot mixture to bowl, stirring constantly. Add egg mixture to the pan and stir constantly until mixture thickens. Remove from heat and cool.

Slice 1 banana into bottom of prepared crust. Pour half of cooled pudding mixture in crust, and top with another sliced banana and the remaining pudding. Slice the last banana on top and spread with whipped cream topping. Chill.

WHIPPED CREAM TOPPING

1 cup heavy cream
½ cup powdered sugar

1 tsp. instant coffee
¼ cup chopped macadamia nuts

In a small bowl, whip cream. Add sugar and coffee. Spread on pie and sprinkle with nuts.

TOFFEE PIE

This pie recipe has been popular for years. For a decorative touch, garnish with chocolate covered coffee beans.

PIE SHELL

1 cup flour
½ tsp. salt
½ cup shortening
⅓ cup brown sugar
¾ cup finely chopped pecans
1 oz. grated unsweetened chocolate
1 tbs. ice water

Combine flour and salt. Cut in shortening until mixture resembles coarse crumbs. Add brown sugar, nuts and chocolate. Sprinkle with ice water and mix well. Pat into a 9-inch pie pan. Bake at 375° for 15 minutes. Cool.

FILLING

¾ cup butter, room temperature
1 cup plus 2 tbs. sugar
1½ oz. unsweetened chocolate,
  melted and cooled

2 tsp. instant coffee powder
3 eggs

Beat butter with an electric mixer until creamy. Gradually add sugar, beating until light. Blend in chocolate and coffee. Add eggs, one at a time, beating for 3 minutes after each addition. Pour into cooled pie shell. Refrigerate several hours or overnight.

TOPPING

1 cup heavy cream
1 tsp. instant coffee powder

¼ cup powdered sugar
1 oz. unsweetened chocolate, grated

Combine cream, coffee and confectioners' sugar in a bowl. Refrigerate several hours. Beat together until stiff and spread on top of pie. Grate chocolate over top.

CREPES BRULOT

Cafe Brulot is a spiced hot coffee drink with strips of lemon and orange peel, which is often flamed tableside. It's a specialty of New Orleans. This dessert is a spin-off of that popular drink.

COFFEE CREPE BATTER

16 crepes

1 cup flour
1½ cups milk
3 eggs
1 tbs. sugar
2 tsp. instant coffee

Blend all ingredients together and strain through a wire mesh sieve. Heat a 6-inch crepe pan or skillet and brush with oil. On medium high heat, pour approximately 2 tbs. of batter into the pan. Lift and twirl skillet to spread. Brown on one side and turn to lightly cook other side. Repeat procedure using remaining batter. Stack crepes using waxed paper to separate.

FILLING

8 oz. cream cheese
1/4 cup powdered sugar
1 tbs. milk

1 tbs. Grand Marnier or brandy
1 tbs. orange zest
1 tsp. lemon zest

Combine ingredients until light and fluffy. Spread on prepared crepes and roll up cigar fashion. Place in a shallow ovenproof casserole. May be refrigerated several hours or overnight at this point.

SAUCE

1/2 cup sugar
2 tbs. cornstarch
2 cups strong brewed coffee
1 tsp. cinnamon

1/4 tsp. cloves
1 tsp. orange zest
1 tsp. lemon zest
1/3 cup brandy

In a saucepan, mix together sugar and cornstarch. Stir in coffee and cook over medium heat, stirring occasionally, until thickened. Add spices and zest. Pour sauce over crepes and bake at 325° until heated through, about 10 to 15 minutes. In a small pan, heat brandy, ignite and pour over crepes. Place crepes on dessert plates, allowing 2 crepes per person. Garnish with whipped cream or ice cream if desired.

SCRUMPTIOUS STUFF CHOCOLATE CREPES WITH KAHLUA MOUSSE

Servings: 12

My friend Sandy is the creator of this elegant recipe that not only tastes delicious but can be made ahead and frozen. She used to have her own catering company called Scrumptious Stuff — and it was.

CHOCOLATE CREPES

24 crepes

4 eggs
1½ cups milk
1 cup flour
¼ cup unsweetened cocoa

¼ cup sugar
2 tsp. vanilla
¼ cup melted butter

Combine ingredients in a food processor using the steel blade or in a blender. Pour batter through a sieve into a pitcher. Heat a crepe pan or skillet over medium high heat and brush lightly with oil. Pour a small amount of batter into the pan, lift and twirl skillet to spread. Cook on one side and turn to cook lightly on other side. Repeat procedure using remaining batter. Stack crepes using waxed paper to separate.

KAHLUA MOUSSE

6 egg yolks
½ cup sugar
1 tbs. Kahlua
2 tsp. instant coffee
3 cups semisweet chocolate chips, melted
1½ cups heavy cream, whipped

Using an electric mixer, beat egg yolks, sugar, Kahlua and coffee until light. Fold in melted chocolate and whipped cream.

TO ASSEMBLE

Spread several spoonfuls of mousse onto one edge of each crepe and roll up cigar fashion. Place in a shallow container and separate layers with waxed paper. May be refrigerated or frozen at this point. If frozen, thaw in the refrigerator before serving. To serve, place two crepes on a pretty dessert plate and garnish with a flower or serve with whipped cream or a sauce. Sauces which go well include hot fudge, raspberry, *Creme Anglaise* or *White Chocolate*, both on page 139.

CHOCOLATE SATIN

This recipe is very versatile in that it can be baked and served as a very rich torte or it can be used unbaked as a filling or frosting. Don't attempt to make it without a food processor.

8 oz. unsweetened chocolate
4 oz. semisweet chocolate
1/2 cup water

1 1/3 cups sugar
1 cup butter, cubed
5 large eggs, room temperature

Preheat oven to 350° and butter a 9-inch cake pan. Line with baking parchment and butter paper. Place sugar and water in a small saucepan and bring to a boil. Stir until sugar dissolves. In a food processor, using the steel blade, combine chocolates and chop finely. With the machine running, add boiling sugar syrup, scraping sides of work bowl. With the machine running, add eggs and butter, processing until mixture is smooth and satiny.

Pour batter into prepared pan and bake for 25 minutes. Cool. Serve cut in wedges with whipped cream, raspberry sauce or *Creme Anglaise*, page 139. Can also be used as a filling or frosting. Refrigerate or freeze any leftovers.

BREADS, MUFFINS AND COFFEE CAKES

BEST EVER CINNAMON ROLLS

We love the hint of orange in these delightful rolls, just the thing to start your morning right with your favorite cup of coffee.

DOUGH

2 pkg. active dry yeast
1/4 cup warm water
1 1/2 cups buttermilk
3 tbs. sugar

1 tsp. salt
1/2 tsp. soda
1/2 cup oil
4 1/2 cups flour

Using the steel blade of a food processor, combine yeast, water and sugar. Process briefly and let stand 5 minutes. Heat buttermilk to lukewarm. Add to work bowl along with half of the flour. Process to combine, letting the machine run for 1 minute. Add salt, soda, oil and remaining flour to the work bowl. Process to make smooth dough. Place dough in an oiled bowl and cover. Let rise 15 minutes.

FILLING

¾ cup butter, melted
2 cups brown sugar

2 tsp. cinnamon
zest of 2 oranges

Combine filling ingredients. Roll dough out on a lightly floured surface into a rectangle approximately 10x18 inches. Spread filling on dough. Roll up lengthwise and cut into twelve 1½-inch pieces. Place cut side up in a buttered 9x13-inch pan. Let rise 30 minutes.

Preheat oven to 400°. Bake rolls for 10 to 15 minutes, until lightly browned. Turn upside down onto a serving platter. Glaze if desired. Serve warm.

GLAZE

4 oz. butter
3 oz. cream cheese

2 cups powdered sugar
juice of 2 oranges

Combine butter, cream cheese and powdered sugar adding orange juice until mixture is of spreading consistency. Drizzle onto warm rolls.

FOOD PROCESSOR BLACK BREAD

1 loaf

This hearty bread goes wonderfully with soups. I've been making bread in my food processor for years and have always been pleased with the results. If your machine seems unable to handle the dough, just finish it by hand and increase kneading time. This recipe can be doubled.

1 cup warm water (115°)
1 pkg. active dry yeast
1 tsp. sugar
1½ cups flour
1 tsp. salt
1 cup whole bran cereal
½ cup strong coffee
2 tbs. distilled vinegar
2 tbs. molasses
1 oz. unsweetened chocolate, melted
2 tbs. butter
2 to 2½ cups rye flour
1 to 2 tbs. caraway seeds

Using the steel blade of the food processor, combine water, yeast and sugar. Process a few seconds and let yeast proof for 5 minutes. Add 1½ cups flour and let the machine run for several minutes to activate gluten in flour.

Add salt, bran, coffee, vinegar, molasses, chocolate, butter and half of the rye flour. Let machine run until a stiff dough forms. Add caraway seeds and remaining flour until dough forms a ball. Remove dough from work bowl and knead on a floured board until dough is smooth and elastic. Put dough into an oiled bowl and turn to coat. Cover with a damp towel and let rise in a warm place until doubled.

Punch down dough and shape into a ball. Place in a greased 8-inch round cake pan and let rise in a warm place until doubled, about 1 hour. Preheat oven to 350°. Bake loaf for 45 minutes or until it sounds hollow when tapped on the bottom.

Prepare glaze: Mix 1 tsp. cornstarch with ⅓ cup water and brush on top of loaf. Return to oven for 3 minutes longer. Remove from pan and cool on a wire rack.

BUTTER PECAN MUFFINS

1 dozen

This recipe is different as the batter is prepared the night before and refrigerated overnight, which makes these ideal for weekend brunches.

½ cup butter
1 cup brown sugar, firmly packed
1 egg
1 cup milk
½ tsp. soda
1 tsp. vanilla
2 cups flour
½ cup chopped pecans

Generously grease a 12-cup muffin tin. Mix ingredients together using an electric mixer. Pour into prepared tin. Cover with plastic wrap and refrigerate overnight.

Preheat oven to 400° Bake muffins for 30 minutes or until done.

MOCHA CHIP MUFFINS

Just the thing for a Sunday morning treat.

½ cup butter
½ cup brown sugar
½ cup granulated sugar
2 tbs. instant coffee
2 tsp. vanilla
2 eggs

⅔ cup milk
1¾ cup flour
½ tsp. salt
1 tbs. baking powder
1 cup semisweet chocolate chips
1 cup chopped walnuts

Preheat oven to 350°. Cream butter, sugars, coffee and vanilla until light and fluffy. Beat together eggs and milk. Sift together flour, salt and baking powder. Add wet ingredients and dry ingredients to butter mixture, stirring just to combine. Add chips and nuts. Line twelve 3-inch muffin cups with paper liners or grease and flour well. Divide batter evenly into muffin tins. Bake for 20 to 25 minutes.

MOM'S RED, WHITE AND BLUE COFFEE CAKE

This recipe is from Christie's mother, a generous hostess and a great cook.

1 cup fresh blueberries
1 cup fresh raspberries
1½ cups sugar
½ cup butter
2 eggs
1 cup sour cream

1 tsp. vanilla
3 cups flour
2 tsp. baking powder
½ tsp. salt
topping, page 93

In a small bowl, gently combine berries and set aside. If fresh berries are not available, use frozen berries, thawed and drained. Using an electric mixer, combine sugar, butter and eggs until light. Add sour cream and vanilla. Sift together dry ingredients and add to butter mixture. Prepare topping. Preheat over to 375° Grease and flour a 9x13-inch pan. Pour ½ batter into prepared pan and top with ½ of the berries. Top with remaining batter and remaining berries and sprinkle with topping. Bake for 1 hour, or until cake tests done. Cool and cut into squares.

TOPPING

1 cup sugar
2/3 cup flour
1/2 cup butter

1 tsp. cinnamon
1/2 tsp. nutmeg
1/2 tsp. salt

Mix topping ingredients together until crumbly. Use the steel knife of a food processor or two knives.

COCONUT SOUR CREAM COFFEE CAKE
Servings: 12

Sour cream makes the cake rich and tender.

1 cup butter
2 cups sugar
3 eggs
1 cup sour cream
1 tsp. vanilla
2 cups flour

1 tsp. baking powder
½ tsp. salt
1½ cups coconut
filling, below

Preheat oven to 325°. Grease and flour a bundt pan. Using an electric mixer, combine butter, sugar and eggs until light. Add sour cream and vanilla. Sift flour, baking soda and salt. Add to creamed mixture. Stir in coconut. Spoon ⅓ of cake batter into prepared pan. Sprinkle with ½ of the filling. Repeat, ending with cake batter. Bake for 1¼ to 1½ hours, or until cake tests done.

FILLING

1 cup chopped pecans
4 tsp. cinnamon

⅓ cup brown sugar
¾ cup coconut

In a small bowl, combine ingredients.

UP ALL NIGHT COFFEE CAKE

Servings: 8 to 10

Fortunately it's the cake that stays up all night — not you. This is so convenient to make the night before a special weekend breakfast. Either the instant or regular pudding mix works well.

¾ cup chopped pecans
1 pkg. (3 lb.) frozen bread dough rolls
1 pkg.(3¾ oz.) butterscotch pudding mix, dry
½ cup brown sugar
½ cup butter, melted
2 tsp. cinnamon

Butter a 10-inch tube pan or bundt pan well. Sprinkle with chopped nuts. Combine dry pudding mix, sugar, butter and cinnamon. Arrange rolls in the pan. Sprinkle with pudding mixture, distributing it evenly. Cover top of pan with plastic wrap and place in a cold oven overnight. In the morning, remove rolls from the oven and preheat oven to 350°. Return rolls to the oven and bake for 25 minutes.

MOCHA COFFEE CAKE
WITH COFFEE GLAZE

Servings: 12 to 16

Just the right touch for a special brunch on Sunday morning. Be sure to feature plenty of freshly brewed coffee to go with it — we particularly like Sulawesi.

BATTER

¾ cup butter
1½ cups sugar
2 tsp. vanilla
3 eggs
3 cups flour

1½ tsp. baking powder
1½ tsp. baking soda
½ tsp. salt
2 cups plain yogurt

Preheat oven to 350°. Prepare filling, page 117, and set aside. Grease and flour a 10-inch tube pan or bundt pan and set aside. With an electric mixer, cream butter and sugar until light and fluffy. Stir in vanilla. Add eggs one at a time, beating well after each addition. Sift together dry ingredients and add ⅓ at a time, alternating with yogurt. Batter will be very thick.

Pour ¼ of the batter into prepared pan and sprinkle with ⅓ of the filling. Repeat twice, ending with batter. Bake for 1 hour or until toothpick inserted in the center comes out clean. Cool on a wire rack. Frost with *Coffee Glaze* and sprinkle with chopped walnuts, if desired.

FILLING

3/4 cup brown sugar
3/4 cup raisins
3/4 cup chopped walnuts

2 tbs. cocoa
1 tbs. cinnamon
2 tsp. instant coffee powder

Combine filling ingredients in a small bowl.

COFFEE GLAZE

1 tsp. instant coffee
1 tbs. hot water
6 tbs. butter
4 oz. cream cheese

3/4 cup powdered sugar
1 tsp. vanilla
1 tsp. orange juice
pinch of salt

To make glaze, combine coffee powder in hot water. Beat butter and cream cheese until light. Add cooled coffee mixture and cream cheese, beating until light and fluffy. Add vanilla, orange juice and salt. Beat until very light. Spread decoratively on top and sides of cake. Sprinkle with nuts if desired.

DESSERTS

CHOCOLATE PATÉ

This dessert is ideal for large parties as it can be made weeks in advance and frozen. We enjoy it with a raspberry sauce, creme anglaise, white chocolate sauce or a bit of whipped cream.

1 pint heavy cream
3 egg yolks
16 oz. semisweet chocolate, chopped
½ cup light corn syrup

½ cup butter
⅓ cup powdered sugar
1 tsp. vanilla

Line a loaf pan with plastic wrap. Combine ½ cup of cream with egg yolks in a heavy 3-quart saucepan. Stir in corn syrup, chocolate and butter. Cook over medium heat, stirring until chocolate is melted. Continue to cook an additional 3 minutes, stirring constantly.

Remove from heat and cool to room temperature. Whip remaining cream with powdered sugar and vanilla. Fold evenly into chocolate mixture. Pour into prepared pan. Wrap well and freeze. To serve, slice across loaf and serve with sauce of your choice.

BOULE DE NEIGE

Servings: 6 to 10

Boule de Neige means snowball in French. This is an elegant, dramatic dessert, easy to prepare ahead for a dinner party. To garnish, pipe rosettes of whipped cream over the entire surface, or simply swirl whipped cream in a decorative fashion. It looks splendid garnished with a red rose and served on a crystal or silver platter.

12 oz. semisweet chocolate, chopped
¾ cup freshly brewed strong coffee
1 cup sugar
1½ cups butter
6 eggs, beaten
1 pint heavy cream, for garnish, whipped and sweetened

Preheat oven to 300°. Line a 1½- or 2-quart stainless steel mixing bowl with a single piece of heavy duty foil. Spray with nonstick cooking spray. Make sure there are no tears in the foil.

Melt chocolate with coffee and sugar in a heavy saucepan over medium heat. Stir until sugar is dissolved. Add butter in pieces, whisking to combine. Remove from heat and quickly stir in beaten eggs. Immediately strain mixture into prepared bowl. Place in lower third of oven and bake for 60 to 65 minutes. It will rise, crack and become crusty and dry around edges. Let cool at room temperature and then refrigerate overnight. Dessert will firm as it cools.

To serve, turn the dessert upside down onto a plate. Peel off the foil and trim any edges to make a nice shape. Frost with whipped cream sweetened to taste or pipe entire surface with whipped cream rosettes using a star tip. Chill until serving. To serve, cut into wedges with a hot knife, wiping the blade between slices.

TRIPLE CHOCOLATE BAVARIAN

Servings: 8

Admittedly this recipe takes a bit of skill, but the results are worth it. Read the directions thoroughly and make it the day before your dinner party when you have a bit of extra time.

1 tbs. unflavored gelatin
¼ cup cold water
5 egg yolks
½ cup sugar
1 cup half and half cream, scalded
3 oz. white chocolate, grated
3 oz. milk chocolate, grated
3 oz. semisweet chocolate, grated
1 tsp. instant coffee powder
1½ cups heavy cream, whipped

Brush the inside of a 6-cup soufflé dish with vegetable oil. Soften gelatin in cold water and set aside. Beat egg yolks in sugar with a mixer until pale yellow and mixture forms a ribbon when the beaters are lifted. Gradually whisk half and half into yolk mixture.

Transfer yolk mixture to a saucepan and cook, stirring constantly until mixture thickens and coats a spoon, about 10 to 12 minutes. Remove from heat and whisk in softened gelatin, stirring thoroughly until gelatin completely dissolves.

Place each of the grated chocolates into its own separate bowl. Add ⅓ of the yolk mixture to each bowl and whisk until chocolate melts. Add coffee powder to the semisweet chocolate mixture. Refrigerate each mixture.

Whip cream until stiff. Fold ⅓ of the whipped cream into each of the chocolate mixtures. Pour white chocolate mixture into oiled dish. Tap to eliminate air bubbles. Cover and freeze for 10 minutes to set layer. Repeat steps with milk chocolate layer and then semisweet chocolate. Cover and refrigerate for 4 hours or overnight.

To serve: Rub bottom and sides of soufflé dish with a hot damp towel and invert onto a lightly oiled plate. Cut into wedges. Serve with a raspberry or mocha fudge sauce. Serve immediately.

KAHLUA FLAN

This makes a delightful dessert for a Mexican meal — or any meal.

2 cups sugar
1/4 cup water
8 eggs

1/2 cup sugar
3 cups whole milk
1 cup Kahlua liqueur

Heat 2 cups of sugar and water in a small saucepan over medium high heat for 25 minutes or until sugar is golden brown. Pour caramelized sugar into a shallow glass baking dish, such as a pie plate or ceramic quiche dish.

Beat together eggs, sugar, milk and Kahlua until well blended. Pour into prepared pan.

Preheat oven to 250°. Place flan in a larger baking pan and fill half way up the sides with boiling water. This is called a *bain marie* or water bath. Bake flan for 45 to 60 minutes or until custard is set.

Chill completely. To serve, spoon custard into individual bowls and drizzle with caramel. Garnish with fresh berries and a sprig of mint if desired.

CHOCOLATE BLISS

The combination of chocolate, cream cheese and almond is really bliss!

1 cup sugar
1/2 cup butter
4 eggs
1 1/2 tbs. sour cream

1 1/2 tbs. vanilla
1/2 tsp. salt
1 cup flour
16 oz. semisweet chocolate, melted

Preheat oven to 350°. Using an electric mixer, combine sugar, butter, eggs, sour cream and vanilla until smooth. Add salt and flour. Melt chocolate and add to mixture. Pour into a 9- or 10-inch springform pan lined with parchment paper.

TOPPING

16 oz. cream cheese
1/2 cup butter
2 eggs

1 cup sugar
2 tbs. almond extract

Combine ingredients using the steel blade of a food processor or an electric mixer. Pour cream cheese mixture on top of chocolate mixture and run a knife through both batters, creating large swirls and giving a marbled effect.

Bake for 20 to 30 minutes or until set. Cool completely and store in the refrigerator. Cut into wedges to serve.

FROZEN ESPRESSO MOUSSE

Servings: 4 to 6

Try using different liqueurs, such as amaretto, Frangelico or creme de cacao to change the flavor of this smooth dessert. Rum or brandy are very good too. This is a nice dessert for a dinner party as it must be made ahead.

1 tbs. instant coffee
1 tbs. hot water
4 eggs, separated
½ cup sugar
1 cup whipping cream
3 tbs. Kahlua

Dissolve coffee in hot water and set aside. Beat egg yolks until thick and lemon colored. In a separate bowl, beat egg whites until stiff, adding sugar gradually until glossy. In another bowl, beat cream until stiff. Blend in coffee mixture and liqueur. Fold all three mixtures together gently to combine. Pour into an attractive freezer-proof mold. Cover and freeze. To serve, scoop into small bowls.

VARIATIONS

- Drizzle the top of each serving with additional liqueur.
- Garnish with a rosette of whipped cream and a chocolate covered coffee bean.
- Sprinkle with finely ground coffee and garnish with a fresh flower.
- Serve with hot fudge sauce or chocolate sauce.
- Place individual servings in pretty coffee mugs or demitasse cups before freezing.

COFFEE POTS DE CREME

Servings: 6

You can make superfine sugar at home by processing regular granulated sugar in the food processor with the steel blade.

2½ cups heavy cream, divided
½ cup superfine sugar
3 tbs. instant coffee
2 tsp. vanilla

6 egg yolks
2 tbs. powdered sugar
cinnamon

Scald 2 cups of cream in a heavy saucepan. Stir in coffee and vanilla. In a separate bowl beat egg yolks and superfine sugar until thick and lemon colored. Gradually pour cream into egg mixture, beating constantly.

Preheat oven to 325°. Bring a pan of water to a boil. Place 6 individual pots de creme cups in a shallow pan. Divide cream mixture evenly into them. Pour boiling water half way up the sides to form a *bain marie* (French water bath). Carefully place in oven and bake for 35 minutes. Cool and refrigerate for 3 hours before serving.

Just before serving, whip remaining ½ cup cream with powdered sugar. Use to garnish tops of pots de creme and dust each with cinnamon.

BRANDIED COFFEE VELVET

Servings: 6

Wonderful for after dinner.

2 tbs. instant coffee
¼ cup hot water
¼ cup chocolate syrup
½ cup brandy
1 quart rich vanilla ice cream
whipped cream for garnish

Dissolve coffee in hot water. Add remaining ingredients and combine until smooth. Chill. Pour into frosted glasses to serve and garnish with whipped cream.

AMARETTO AND KAHLUA SEMIFREDDO

This is a wonderful dessert for a busy hostess as it must be made ahead. Semifreddo never freezes completely solid and the contrast in temperatures between the cold dessert and the hot fudge sauce is fantastic.

2 cups heavy cream
1 cup powdered sugar
4 egg whites
¼ cup amaretto liqueur
¼ cup Kahlua liqueur
2 tbs. instant coffee

Prepare a long narrow freezer proof container, such as a bread pan, by lining with plastic wrap. It helps the plastic to stick if you first spray lightly with non-stick cooking spray. In a bowl, whip cream until beginning to thicken, slowly adding powdered sugar. In a separate bowl, whip egg whites until soft peaks form. Fold the two mixtures together. Divide mixture into 2 bowls. Add amaretto to first bowl. Pour into prepared pan and smooth into an even layer. Place in freezer until beginning to set.

Dissolve coffee in 1 tsp. hot water. Add coffee and Kahlua to second bowl. Carefully spread on top of amaretto layer. Cover with plastic and freeze several hours or overnight.

To serve, cut into slices and serve drizzled with warm fudge sauce. If desired, garnish with a dollop of whipped cream and a chocolate-covered espresso bean.

VARIATION

Stir crushed amaretti cookie crumbs into the amaretto layer and grated semisweet chocolate into the Kahlua layer.

COFFEE ALMOND TORTONI

A nice dessert for an Italian meal.

1 cup heavy cream
½ cup sugar, divided
1 tsp. vanilla extract
½ tsp. almond extract

2 egg whites, room temperature
½ cup finely chopped toasted almonds
½ cup flaked toasted coconut
1 tsp. instant coffee powder

Line 8 muffin cups with paper liners. Combine cream with ¼ cup of the sugar, vanilla and almond extract and beat until soft peaks form. In a separate bowl, beat egg whites, gradually adding remaining sugar, until stiff. Fold in whipped cream and ½ of the nuts and coconut. Spoon half of the mixture evenly into muffin tins, smoothing top with back of a spoon. Add coffee powder to remaining whipped cream mixture and spoon an even layer over top of tortoni. Sprinkle tops with remaining almonds and coconuts. Cover and freeze until serving.

ESPRESSO TIRAMISU

Tiramisu means "pick-me-up" in Italian. Mascarpone is a sweet Italian cream cheese. This is a shortened version of this popular dessert.

¾ cup Kahlua
2 cups espresso
50 lady fingers
3¾ cups marscapone cheese

2½ cups heavy cream
1 cup sugar
½ cup cocoa powder

Combine Kahlua and espresso in a large bowl. Dip lady fingers in mixture and use them to line bottom and sides of a 10-inch springform pan, arranging them in an attractive design. You will use about ⅓ of the lady fingers.

Using the steel blade of a food processor, combine mascarpone, cream and sugar until it begins to thicken.

Spread ⅓ of the cheese mixture over the bottom of the pan. Layer again with liqueur-soaked lady fingers. Repeat layers twice, ending with cheese mixture. Dust top with cocoa powder. Cover and chill at least 3 hours or overnight. Remove sides from pan. Cut into wedges to serve.

CRICKET'S AUTHENTIC TIRAMISU

My friend Cricket, who studied cooking in Italy, presents her version of this wonderful dessert. A challenging recipe, but worth the effort and calories involved.

PAN DI SPAGNA (SPONGE CAKE)

4 large eggs, separated
1 tsp. vanilla
¾ cup sugar

½ cup flour
½ cup cornstarch
pinch of salt

Preheat oven to 350°. Butter a 9-or 10-inch cake pan that is 2 inches deep, and line with parchment. Using a mixer, beat egg yolks with vanilla for 5 minutes. Sift flour and cornstarch together. In a separate bowl, using an electric mixer, beat egg whites and salt until they hold a firm peak. Fold yolks into whites. Sift flour and cornstarch into egg mixture in 3 additions. Do not over-mix. Pour batter into prepared pan, smoothing top. Bake for 30 to 40 minutes, or until cake tests done. Gently invert onto a wire rack and cool.

ESPRESSO SYRUP

⅓ cup sugar
¼ cup water

½ cup very strong brewed espresso
¼ cup brandy

Combine sugar and water in a saucepan and bring to a boil. Cool. Add espresso and brandy. Set aside.

ZABAGLIONE FILLING

3 large egg yolks
1/3 cup sugar
1/3 cup sweet Marsala wine

1/2 pound mascarpone cheese, at
room temperature
2/3 cup heavy cream, whipped

Using an electric mixer, beat egg yolks, sugar and marsala until light. Set bowl over a pan of simmering water and continue beating until thickened, about 10 minutes. Whip mascarpone until smooth. Fold together the egg mixture, Mascarpone and whipped cream.

To assemble: Cut sponge cake into 1/4-inch vertical slices. Place a layer slices in a shallow 2-quart dish. Soak with 1/3 of the espresso syrup. Spread with 1/2 of the filling. Repeat layers of cake, syrup, filling, cake and syrup. Spread with topping.

TOPPING

1 cup heavy cream, whipped
2 tbs. sugar
ground cinnamon

ground coffee
unsweetened cocoa powder

Whip cream and sweeten with sugar. Decorate top of tiramisu and dust with cinnamon, coffee and cocoa. Refrigerate several hours before serving.

COFFEE COEUR LA CREME

An unusual twist on the traditional Coeur la Creme. Serve this rich cheese spread with English biscuits, plain cookies or fresh fruit.

16 oz. cream cheese, softened
1 cup heavy cream, whipped
½ cup sour cream
2 tbs. instant coffee
1 tbs. boiling water
3 tbs. powdered sugar

Blend softened cream cheese with whipped cream. Stir in sour cream. Dissolve coffee in water and add to mixture along with powdered sugar. Line a pretty mold with damp cheese cloth and fill with cheese mixture. Chill several hours or overnight. Unmold onto a pretty dessert plate and garnish with fresh flowers.

COFFEE FROMAGE

This is a rich, whipped molded dessert from Norway, very much like a Bavarian cream. Garnish with whipped cream and fresh fruit such as oranges, bananas, strawberries, raspberries or peaches.

1 envelope unflavored gelatin
3 tbs. water
3 eggs
¾ cup sugar
2 tbs. instant coffee powder

1 cup heavy cream
fresh fruit for garnish
sweetened whipped cream, for
   garnish

Soften gelatin in water. Stir over hot water or microwave until dissolved. In the large bowl of an electric mixer, beat eggs until light. Add sugar and instant coffee. Beat at high speed for 5 minutes or until very thick.

Whip cream until stiff. Add dissolved gelatin. Fold mixture into beaten eggs and beat at lowest speed of mixer until well combined. Pour into a 5-cup dessert mold and chill until set, about 4 hours or overnight.

To serve, dip mold into warm water and loosen edges with a knife. Unmold onto a pretty dessert plate and garnish with fresh fruit and whipped cream.

POACHED PEARS WITH MOCHA SABAYON

The combination of chilled fresh pears and rich warm sauce is wonderful!

6 ripe Bartlett pears, with stems
3 cups water
1 cup sugar

1 piece lemon rind
1 stick cinnamon

Peel pears, leaving stems on. In a large saucepan combine water, sugar, lemon and cinnamon. Bring to a boil and add pears. Cover and gently poach until just tender. Test in fattest part of the pear, using the tip of a small knife. Let pears cool in the syrup. Refrigerate until chilled.

SABAYON

4 oz. semisweet chocolate
3/4 cup strong coffee
9 egg yolks

5 tbs. sugar
1/4 cup brandy

Melt chocolate with 1/4 cup of coffee and set aside. In the top of a double boiler, mix egg yolks with sugar and beat with an electric mixer until pale yellow. Do not underbeat! Gradually add melted chocolate and remaining coffee to egg mixture, stirring over simmering water until creamy and thickened. Add brandy. To serve, place pears in individual dessert dishes and spoon sauce over.

COOKIES, CONFECTIONS AND SAUCES

JUAN VALDEZ' FAVORITE COOKIE BARS

2 dozen

These pack well and are ideal for picnics, lunches or hikes.

12 oz. semisweet chocolate chips,
  divided
½ cup butter
1⅓ cups flour
1 tsp. baking powder
1 tsp. salt
5 eggs

3 tsp. instant coffee
1 tsp. hot water
3 tsp. vanilla
1½ cups sugar
1⅓ cups graham cracker crumbs
1½ cups chopped pecans

Melt ½ of the chocolate chips with butter. Cool.

Combine flour, baking powder and salt. With an electric mixer, beat eggs and sugar until light. Dissolve coffee in hot water and add to egg mixture with vanilla. Add chocolate and butter mixture. Mix well. Add flour mixture, crumbs, remaining chocolate chips and nuts. Pour into a greased 9x13-inch baking pan and bake at 350° for 25 to 35 minutes or until a toothpick inserted in the center comes out clean. Frost while still warm.

COFFEE CREAM CHEESE GLAZE

4 oz. cream cheese, softened
2 tbs. butter
3 tsp. instant coffee
1 tsp. hot water
2 cups powdered sugar
1 to 2 tbs. milk

Using the steel blade of a food processor, combine cream cheese and butter until smooth. Dissolve coffee in hot water and add to mixture. Add powdered sugar and beat until light, adding milk as necessary. Frost bars. Cool completely and cut into squares.

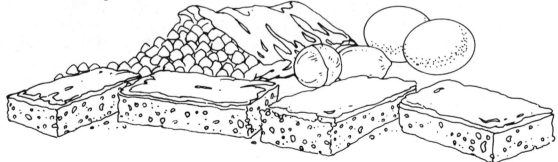

BROWNIE BOMBERS

Change liquors to suit your taste. Try using rum or brandy on the base and creme de menthe or Bailey's Irish Creme in the center.

BROWNIE BASE

2 cups sugar
1 cup butter
4 eggs
4 oz. unsweetened chocolate, melted
2 tsp. instant coffee
2 tsp. vanilla

2½ cups flour
¼ tsp. salt
¼ tsp. baking powder
1 cup walnuts or pecans, coarsely
   chopped
¼ cup bourbon

Preheat oven to 325°. Cream butter, sugar and eggs. Add melted chocolate, coffee and vanilla. Stir in flour, salt, baking powder and nuts. Spread into a well-greased 9x13-inch pan and bake for 30 minutes. Remove from oven and drizzle with bourbon while hot. Refrigerate.

BUTTER CREAM LAYER

1 cup butter
3 tbs. Kahlua
2 cups powdered sugar

Mix until fluffy and spread on cooled brownies. Chill.

CHOCOLATE GLAZE

6 oz. semisweet chocolate chips
1 tsp. instant coffee
1 tbs. vegetable shortening

Melt chocolate and coffee with shortening. Spread on top of butter cream layer. Chill.

MOCHA MELTAWAYS

Similar to a Naniamo Bar, these rich bars literally melt in your mouth.

CRUST

1½ cups graham cracker crumbs
1½ cups chocolate wafer crumbs
1 cup chopped walnuts

½ cup melted butter
¼ cup sugar
1 tbs. vanilla

Combine ingredients and press into bottom of a 9x13-inch pan. Chill.

MOCHA BUTTERCREAM

4 oz. white chocolate, melted
½ cup butter
1 cup powdered sugar

2 eggs
1 tbs. instant coffee
1 tsp. hot water

Using the steel blade of a food processor, or an electric mixer, combine butter and powdered sugar until smooth. Add eggs and melted white chocolate. Dissolve coffee in hot water and add to mixture. Spread on prepared crust.

Top with a layer of *Chocolate Satin*, page 79. Freeze any extra topping for another recipe. Store in refrigerator or freeze. Cut into bars to serve.

FUDGE FROGGIES

18 bars

These delectable bars are a cross between fudge and a brownie. Our all-time favorite brownie.

1 lb. semisweet chocolate chips
1 cup butter, cut in pieces
1/3 cup strong brewed coffee
4 large eggs, room temperature

1½ cups sugar
½ cup flour
2 cups coarsely chopped walnuts

Melt together chocolate, butter and coffee. In an electric mixer, beat eggs and sugar until light. Slowly add chocolate mixture. With a spoon, stir in flour and walnuts.

Preheat oven to 375°. Line a 9x13-inch baking pan with foil. Generously butter foil. Pour batter into prepared pan. Bake for 30 minutes or until just set around edges. Cool on a wire rack for 30 minutes. Cover pan with foil and refrigerate for several hours or overnight.

Cut into bars to serve. Best stored in refrigerator.

MOCHA ALMOND FLORENTINES

Servings: 30

Using disposable aluminum cake or tartlet pans makes clean up easy. The technique is bit time-consuming but the results are worth it.

1 cup butter
1 cup sugar
6 tbs. honey
6 tbs. heavy cream

1 lb. slivered blanched almonds
3 tsp. instant coffee
1 tsp. hot water
12 oz. semisweet chocolate

Preheat oven to 375°. Spray six 8-inch round foil cake pans or thirty 3-inch tartlet pans with nonstick cooking spray. In a heavy saucepan, combine butter, sugar, honey and cream. Bring to a boil over medium heat, stirring frequently. Cook at a boil for 1½ minutes, stirring constantly. Remove from heat and add almonds. Divide mixture evenly into prepared pans, using your fingers dipped in cold water to flatten. If using individual tartlet pans, place them on cookie sheets. Bake for 10 to 12 minutes or until golden around the edges. Let cookies cool in the pans; they will harden as they cool. Place pans in the freezer for 10 minutes. Remove cookies by tapping and gently pressing on backs of pans.

Combine instant coffee and hot water. Melt chocolate and stir in coffee mixture. With a spoon, spread chocolate on the back of each cookie. Place upside down on wire racks to harden. Store in refrigerator or freezer.

ESPRESSO SHORTBREAD

If you wish, melt semisweet chocolate and dip each cookie one third of the way up in the melted chocolate. Press a blanched almond or pecan half in the center of each.

1 cup butter
½ cup brown sugar, firmly packed
1 tsp. vanilla
¾ tsp. instant coffee
2¼ cups flour
¼ tsp. salt

Cream butter and sugar until fluffy. Add vanilla and coffee. Combine flour and salt and add to mixture. Chill dough. Preheat oven to 325°. Roll dough to ¼-inch thickness. Cut into bars 1 inch wide and 3 inches long. Prick with a fork. Place on greased cookie sheets and bake for 20 to 25 minutes or until golden.

OLD-FASHIONED
MOLASSES SPICE COOKIES

6 dozen

This treasured family recipe has been handed down through the generations by Helen Louise Thwing. She was nice enough to share it with us. Try it in your lunch box — it makes a big batch.

1 cup butter
1 cup brown sugar
1 cup molasses
2 eggs
1 cup strong coffee
1 lb. dark raisins

4 cups flour
1 tbs. *each* cinnamon, cloves, ginger
1½ tsp. baking soda
1 tsp. nutmeg
1 tsp. salt
¼ tsp. allspice

In a large mixing bowl, cream butter, brown sugar, molasses and eggs until fluffy. Pour hot coffee over raisins and let plump. Stir together flour and spices. Add to creamed mixture. Combine with undrained raisins. Preheat oven to 350198. Drop dough by rounded teaspoons onto greased baking sheets. Bake for 15 minutes. Cool on wire racks. If desired, frost with *Browned Butter Icing*.

BROWNED BUTTER ICING

½ cup butter
3 to 4 cups powdered sugar
1 tsp. vanilla

In a saucepan, heat butter until just beginning to brown. It should give off a very "nutty" aroma. Remove from heat and add powdered sugar until spreading consistency. Stir in vanilla. Spread on cooled cookies.

MOCHA MACADAMIA NUT COOKIES

4 dozen

These flavorful cookies are similar to chocolate chip cookies, with the addition of coffee, macadamia nuts and white chocolate chips. Be sure to chill the dough well and don't overbake.

1 cup butter
1¾ cups brown sugar
2 eggs
½ cup brewed strong coffee
3½ cups flour
1 tsp. baking soda

1 tsp. nutmeg
½ tsp. salt
½ tsp. cinnamon
1 cup semisweet chocolate chips
1 cup white chocolate chips
1 cup macadamia nuts

Cream butter, sugar, eggs and coffee until fluffy. Sift flour, soda, salt and spices and add to mixture. Stir in chips and nuts. Chill dough well for at least 1 hour. To bake, preheat oven to 400°. Drop dough by rounded spoonfuls onto greased baking sheets. Bake until edges are light brown, about 8 to 10 minutes. Remove to wire racks to cool. Store in a covered container.

MEXICAN MOCHA BALLS

3 dozen

These delightful little cookies are similar to the familiar Mexican tea cakes or wedding balls.

1 cup butter
½ cup sugar
1 tsp. vanilla
2 cups flour
1 tsp. instant coffee
½ tsp. salt
1 cup chopped walnuts
½ cup chopped maraschino cherries, well drained

Combine butter, sugar and vanilla. Add flour, coffee and salt. Stir in walnuts and cherries. Chill dough 1 hour. Form chilled dough into 1-inch balls and place on an ungreased cookie sheet. Preheat oven to 325°. Bake cookies for 20 minutes. Cool on a wire rack. Roll in powdered sugar and store in an air-tight container.

MOCHA MADELEINES

These charming little cookies are perfect for an afternoon tea.

melted butter for molds
2 oz. semisweet chocolate
½ cup butter
2 eggs
¼ cup sugar
1 tsp. vanilla
1 tsp. instant coffee

1 tsp. hot water
½ tsp. brandy
½ cup cake flour
2 tsp. cocoa
½ tsp. baking powder
powdered sugar

Preheat oven to 325°. Brush madeleine molds with butter. Melt chocolate with ½ cup butter. Beat eggs with sugar until thick. Add melted chocolate mixture, vanilla, coffee, water and brandy. Stir in flour, cocoa and baking powder, mixing until flour just disappears. Spoon batter into prepared molds, filling ⅔ full. Bake for 10 to 12 minutes or until a toothpick inserted in the center is clean. Loosen cookies and invert over a cake rack. Cool to room temperature. Dust with powdered sugar sprinkled through a sieve. Arrange the cookies on your prettiest plate and garnish with flowers.

ORANGE ALMOND BISCOTTI

3 dozen

Biscotti are baked twice. The key to success is not to bake them too long the first time, so they will slice nicely for the second baking. I can't imagine why people buy expensive biscotti when they are so easy and fun to do at home.

½ cup butter
1 cup sugar
2 eggs
1 tsp. orange zest
1 tsp. almond extract

1¾ cups flour
1½ cups ground almonds
1 cup whole almonds, blanched,
    toasted and coarsely chopped

Preheat oven to 350. Cream butter, sugar, eggs, orange zest and extract until light and fluffy. Stir in flour, salt and nuts. Dough will be soft. On a floured board with floured hands, shape dough into four 1-inch logs. Use additional flour as needed. Transfer logs to greased cookie sheets, leaving 3 inches of space between logs. Bake logs for 10 to 12 minutes, until firm. Do not over-bake. Remove sheets from oven. Turn oven to 275°. As soon as logs are cool enough to handle, cut on a 45° angle into ½-inch slices using a bread knife. Return to baking sheet and bake 10 minutes or until biscotti are dry. Transfer to wire racks to cool.

MOCHA SPICE BISCOTTI

3 dozen

These biscotti are for sophisticated taste buds only — they have a spicy bite!

1/2 cup butter
1/2 cup brown sugar
1/2 cup granulated sugar
2 eggs
1 tsp. vanilla
1 tsp. almond extract
1 cup ground almonds
2 cups flour

1/4 tsp. salt
1 tsp. white pepper
1 tsp. ground ginger
2 tbs. instant coffee
4 oz. semisweet chocolate, melted
1 cup whole almonds, blanched and toasted

Preheat oven to 350°. Grease 2 cookie sheets. Cream butter, sugars, eggs and extract until light. Stir in ground nuts, flour, spices, coffee and melted chocolate. Mix well. Fold in toasted almonds. On a floured board, pat dough into a large flat round. Divide in quarters. Roll each quarter into a 1-inch log. Transfer logs to prepared baking sheet, Leaving 3 inches of space between. Bake for 10 to 15 minutes or until firm. Remove sheets from oven and cool.

Turn oven to 275°. Slice logs on a sharp 45° angle 1/2-inch thick using a bread knife. Return to baking sheets and bake for 15 to 20 minutes or until biscotti are dry. Transfer to wire racks to cool.

MOCHA NUT BALLS

These freeze beautifully and make a lovely Christmas gift.

1 pkg. (12 oz.) semisweet chocolate chips
4 egg yolks
1½ cups powdered sugar
1 cup butter
3 tsp. instant coffee
4 tbs. brandy
2 tsp. vanilla
2 cups finely chopped toasted nuts (pecans, almonds or walnuts)

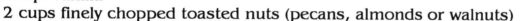

Melt chocolate and let cool. Using an electric mixer, beat egg yolks and sugar until smooth. Add butter a little at a time. Dissolve coffee in brandy and add egg-butter mixture with vanilla. Add chocolate and mix thoroughly. Chill in a shallow dish. Using a melon baller or teaspoon, shape into small balls and roll in chopped nuts. Refrigerate or freeze. Bring to room temperature before serving.

FOOD PROCESSOR TRUFFLES

These make a nice gift from your kitchen at holiday time. A variety of liqueurs and coatings can be used. This recipe makes about 40 one-inch truffles. For the adventuresome, you can even try hand-dipping these in melted chocolate. Be sure to let the truffles sit at room temperature for 30 minutes before eating, so they will develop their full flavor and aroma.

½ pound semisweet chocolate chips
½ cup strong brewed coffee
1 tbs. butter
1 tbs. liqueur of your choice
½ cup unsweetened cocoa or topping of your choice

Using the steel blade of a food processor, chop chocolate very fine. Heat coffee until just below boiling. With machine running, pour coffee down the feed tube. Add butter and liqueur and scrape sides of the work bowl. Continue processing until well combined and smooth. Put processor bowl into the refrigerator and chill until mixture is firm enough to be shaped.

Form into small balls using a melon ball scoop, a teaspoon or your hands. Roll in cocoa. Store in a covered container well sealed in the refrigerator for up to 2 weeks. May be frozen for up to 3 months.

Liqueur Suggestions

amaretto
bourbon
brandy
Kahlua

Frangelico
kirsch
rum

Coating Suggestions

chopped nuts: walnuts, pecans,
  almonds or hazelnuts
coconut

chocolate sprinkles
crushed amaretti crumbs
cocoa

Toppings

chocolate coffee beans
candied violets

candied citrus rind

COFFEE ICE CREAM BONBONS

30 bonbons

These are something special to offer with after-dinner coffee. Experiment with using other liqueurs and flavors of ice cream.

1 tbs. unflavored gelatin
2 tbs. water
3 tbs. Kahlua or other liqueur
1 quart coffee ice cream, softened
4 oz. semisweet chocolate chips
1 oz. vegetable shortening

In a small saucepan, soften gelatin in water and dissolve over low heat. Cool and add liqueur. Using an electric mixer, combine ice cream and gelatin mixture. Pour into a metal pan and freeze several hours or overnight.

To form bonbons, chill a cookie sheet in the freezer. Using a melon baller, quickly form small ice cream balls. Place on chilled cookie sheet and insert a frilled toothpick into each. Return bonbons to freezer until firm.

Melt chocolate and shortening, stirring well. Pour into a coffee cup and cool slightly. Dip ice cream balls into chocolate, coating thoroughly. Return to freezer.

WHITE CHOCOLATE SAUCE

1½ cups

Perfect as a sauce for Chocolate Paté, page 85. For a change of pace use Grand Marnier or Frangelico instead of Kahlua. It keeps well.

1 cup heavy cream   ½ cup Kahlua
9 oz. white chocolate, grated

Scald cream and remove from heat. Whisk in white chocolate. Pour into a food processor fitted with the steel blade and process until smooth. Add liqueur.

CREME ANGLAISE

2½ cups

This rich custard sauce may be flavored with your favorite liqueur or finely chopped toasted macadamia nuts or almonds.

2 cups heavy cream   pinch of salt
6 egg yolks   2 tbs. liqueur of your choice, optional
½ cup sugar

Heat cream in a saucepan but do not boil. Whisk together egg yolks, sugar and salt until light yellow. Add cream and mix to blend. Pour mixture into a double boiler and cook until thickened.

MOCHA FUDGE SAUCE

1 cup

This sauce can easily be doubled. Store leftovers in a jar in the refrigerator. Try it over the Amaretto and Kahlua Semifreddo dessert, page 96. Today's food stylists often serve the dessert on top of the sauce or drizzle it over the top in a zig zag pattern.

3 tbs. butter
3 oz. unsweetened chocolate
½ cup strong coffee
¼ cup light corn syrup
1 cup sugar
1 tsp. vanilla

In a saucepan, melt butter and chocolate. Stir in remaining ingredients except vanilla. Bring sauce to a boil and continue boiling gently, without stirring, until thick and smooth, about 10 minutes. Add vanilla. Serve sauce immediately or store in the refrigerator.

PART II - TEA

For centuries, people all over the world have found comfort, communication and warmth in a simple cup of tea. The traditions, ceremonies and politics of tea have impacted civilization throughout history. In this section, you will find a bit of information about tea as well as recipes we find particularly good with tea. So whether you're enjoying a solitary cup or planning a festive party, you'll find something delicious to go with your next cup.

THE HISTORY OF TEA

Next to water, tea is the most popular drink in the world. Its history dates back almost 5,000 years. Although no one knows for certain how tea drinking began, legend has it that the Chinese Emperor, Shen Nung, was drinking hot water under a tree one day when a leaf from a nearby bush drifted into his cup. One sip and he was hooked! Supposedly this took place around 2737 B.C. At that time, tea leaves were dried, powdered and stirred into hot water. They were also made into cakes and added to boiled rice with spices and nuts. It wasn't until the Ming Dynasty, 1368 to 1644 A.D., that tea leaves were brewed as an infusion, as we know it today.

Tea was introduced to Japan by Buddhist priests in 593 A.D. It was the Dutch who brought green tea from Japan to Europe in the early 1600s. Initially it was sold for medicinal purposes and as an expensive drink, enjoyed only by the very wealthy. In the late 1700s the economy changed, reducing the price so that tea could be enjoyed by all.

In America, tea was the beverage of choice until the Revolution. When the British passed the Tea Act of 1773 the Colonists boycotted tea completely. A group of Colonists, dressed as Indians, threw the tea from three ships into the harbor in what is known as the Boston Tea Party.

After the revolution tea became popular again, and the trade between China and America flourished. Great fortunes were made as ships from the Atlantic ports sailed around Cape Horn to the Pacific Northwest. There they loaded their ships with furs to trade in the Orient for tea, silk and spices.

Both iced tea and the tea bag are fairly recent American inventions. Iced tea was first served at the World's Fair in St. Louis in 1901. Temperatures were soaring, and when an enterprising tea salesman poured tea over ice, the crowds loved it. We've been drinking iced tea ever since and today over 80 percent of the domestic tea market in the United States is served as iced tea.

In New York in 1908 another enterprising tea salesman began sending his samples to retailers in small silk bags. Assuming the tea was to be steeped in the bags, the retailers put them right into their pots. They loved the convenience of the premeasured, self-straining bags and ordered more!

Today, Americans use over 200 million pounds of tea per year. Most of it comes from China, India and Sri Lanka. The United Kingdom imports almost twice that amount.

HOW TEA IS GROWN

The tea plant is a member of the camellia family. It is an evergreen which grows in tropical and subtropical climates. Even though there is a tea plantation in South Carolina and isolated plants have been grown in other areas, tea plants need rain in order to flourish. A climate with 50 inches of annual rainfall is ideal for growing tea. Much like the grapes used to make wine take on certain characteristics of the soil and climate, the tea plant also takes on a distinct flavor from the climate and soil in which it is grown. For example, a tea plant growing in India will taste completely different if transplanted to China.

If left unpruned, a tea plant will grow to a height of over 50 feet. Most plants are pruned, trained and clipped to a flat surface for ease in picking and are about four feet tall. Pruning also keeps the bush from going to seed and keeps it in a vegetative state where it produces new leaves year after year. A tea plant may remain productive for over a century!

Most tea plants are propagated by cuttings. Tea is a monoculture — that is, a crop grown in the same location year after year — so fertilizing is very important to maintain a healthy crop. On a typical tea estate there are usually 3000 to 5000 bushes per acre. Each acre yields 1000 to 2000 pounds of leaf per year.

The young leaf shoots and the unopened leaf buds of the tea plant are responsible for the smell and taste of the tea. There are two categories of picking — *fine* and *coarse*. These refer to the size of the shoot that is plucked. Two leaves and a bud are considered fine plucking and three or more is considered coarse. High quality teas are always harvested with fine plucking, the premium leaves. Tea is plucked or harvested at least three times a year, and in some climates it is a continual process. The frequency of picking depends on the number of new growths or flushes as they are called. There is a delicate balance between the frequency and the fineness of plucking, fertilizing and pruning in order to produce the maximum growth and quality.

Picking tea is almost always done by hand. A large tea estate will employ several hundred workers, most of them women. It takes 2000 to 3000 shoots to produce one pound of tea. The average worker will pick about 800 pounds of tea per year.

TEA PROCESSING

All tea falls into one of three categories: *green*, *black* or *oolong*. These divisions are based solely on the methods of processing the tea leaf. Virtually all Japanese tea is green, almost all Indian tea is black, and China produces all three. Most Americans prefer black teas.

Green tea is the simplest process. Shortly after the leaves are plucked, they are steamed or heated to stop the enzymatic action. The leaf is softened by the heat and then rolled various ways - balled, flat, curly, thin or twisted.

Drying reduces the moisture content of the leaf, preventing any further chemical changes. When brewing, boiling water meets the tea and releases the natural fragrance and flavor that were stabilized during the steaming and drying process.

Black teas are dried out so that they lose about half of their moisture content. This process is called *withering*. The fresh green leaves are spread out on tiered racks of heavy cloth. Sometimes these withering lofts are several stories high. Another method involves placing the leaves in wire mesh trough. If the climate is not too wet or humid, the leaves dry naturally. Otherwise, huge fans are used. After the leaves are withered, they are taken to huge rolling machines. Each machine holds several hundred pounds of leaves. These machines twist and roll the leaves, breaking down their cellular structure and releasing the juices. The enzymatic action begins and the leaves darken. Then the leaves are broken up by coarse sieves, or roll breakers. Next the leaves move to the fermenting rooms, where they are spread out to ferment and develop their full fragrance. This takes anywhere from twenty minutes to three hours. Briefly, this step occurs when the enzymes and oxygen combine to give the tea leaves their bright color. It also mellows the flavor of the juices, which prior to this point have been astringent and bitter. After the fermentation, the leaves are dried in huge chambers until they turn black and have a moisture content of about 5%.

Basically, this is the key distinction between green teas and black teas. Green teas are called unfermented and black teas are called fermented.

Oolong teas are prepared much like black tea but are given only the briefest withering period and are only partially oxidized. Thus they share some of the same characteristics of both green and black teas.

THE SORTING AND GRADING OF TEA

Grading tea is a matter of size rather than quality of the leaves. After the black and oolong teas are dried, they are sorted into grades by machines. Different sizes are separated by vibrating wire mesh screens. It's important that the tea be consistent in size as smaller pieces brew more quickly than large ones. The two grades of tea are *leaf grades* and *broken grades*.

Leaf grades include: *souchong*, *pekoe* and *orange pekoe*.

Broken grades include: *broken pekoe souchong*, *broken pekoe*, *broken orange pekoe*, *fannings* and *dust*.

Green tea is graded according to the age of leaves and preparation. Some of the varieties include *gunpowder*, *imperial* and *hyson*.

VARIETIES OF TEA

Teas are often named for the area in which they are grown, such as Ceylon or Kenya. As many as 20 or 30 different teas will go into a blend. Here are some of the most common varieties:

Blended teas. Various teas are combined to enhance a particular characteristic or flavor. Earl Grey, English Breakfast and China Caravan are familiar examples of blended tea.

Scented and flavored teas. Teas which have been enhanced by flowers, natural oils or fruits. Jasmine, Lychee, Lemon and Almond are popular varieties.

Spiced tea. As the name suggests, these teas are often flavored with cinnamon or other combinations of spices.

Herbal teas. Often these mixtures contain no tea at all, but are infusions or tisanes of various flowers, leaves, stems and herbs. Certain herbs are thought to have medicinal properties, such as chamomile for sleep or ginseng for potency.

Decaffeinated tea. Water is the preferred method to decaffeinated tea. The chemicals used to decaffeinate coffee are restricted by law for use in decaffeinating tea. Sometimes ethyl acetate is used, but it adversely effects the tea.

THE PROPER POT, OR HOW TO BREW TEA

A perfect cup of tea begins with your favorite high quality tea. Use fresh cold tap water. Bring the kettle to a rolling boil. Preheat your teapot by rinsing with very hot tap water. Purists bring the pot to the kettle, never the kettle to the pot. Pour the water directly onto the tea. Cover with the lid and let the tea steep for 3 to 5 minutes. Tea releases its color long before its flavor, so its color is no indication of the proper strength. If the resulting brew is too strong for your personal liking, there are two schools of thought. One is to use less tea, the other is to add more hot water.

Just before pouring, stir the tea to evenly distribute the flavor. Any tea left in the pot for longer than 10 minutes will develop an off flavor if the leaves are not removed. Either remove the leaves using a perforated spoon or strain into another warmed teapot.

To add milk to tea is a matter of continuing debate. In England it is common practice. Milk is only used with black tea, never green tea or oolong. The milk neutralizes the tannins in the tea and reduces the astringency. Cream should never be used in tea as the fat content changes the flavor. Some like a bit of lemon, sugar or honey in their tea, but it is mostly a matter of personal taste.

Be sure to keep your teapot clean, but avoid using a detergent that might leave a residue. The best way to clean a teapot is to fill it with hot water and a tablespoon of baking soda and let it stand for several hours.

TEA BEVERAGES

LIME TEA

This is a refreshing beverage to serve with a Mexican meal.

2 cups boiling water
2 tbs. loose tea
1/2 cup sugar
2 1/2 cups ginger ale

2 1/2 cups lemon lime soda
peel from two limes
1/2 cup lime juice
1/2 cup corn syrup

Pour the boiling water over tea and steep for 5 minutes. Strain. Add sugar and lime skins and let stand for 1 hour. Remove skins from tea and add remaining ingredients. Serve chilled over ice.

MAUI ICED TEA

Servings: 8 to 12

Just before this book was published, our family enjoyed a wonderful vacation in Hawaii, where we picked up several new recipes which we wanted to share.

2 quarts brewed tea
1 cup orange juice
1 cup lime juice

1 cup pineapple juice
1/2 cup guava juice
sugar to taste, start with 1/3 cup

Combine all ingredients and serve over ice.

SPECIAL ICED TEA

16 cups

This is a nice make-ahead drink to have on hand for those hot summer days.

2 cups water
2 cups sugar
1 quart hot water
8 tea bags

2 quarts cold water
2 cups orange juice
¾ cup lemon juice

Combine 2 cups water and sugar in a large saucepan and boil 5 minutes. Remove from heat and add 1 quart hot water and tea bags. Steep tea bags for 3 to 5 minutes, according to strength desired. Add cold water, orange and lemon juice. Refrigerate or serve immediately over ice and garnish each glass with a slice of orange and a sprig of fresh mint.

GINGER TEA

6 cups

Try this for a change of pace.

4 slices ginger root, ¼-inch thick
¼ cup light brown sugar

6 cups boiling water

Bruise ginger slices with flat side of a large knife blade. Place ginger in teapot and add sugar and water. Steep 5 minutes.

PARTY PUNCH

This refreshing punch is perfect for a patio or backyard party.

1 tsp. whole cloves
4 cups strong brewed tea, such as Earl Grey
4 cups brewed mint tea
1 quart pineapple juice
1 quart orange juice
1 quart apple juice
½ cup lemon juice
2 liters ginger ale
1 fifth light rum
orange, lemon and lime slices for garnish
fresh mint sprigs

Steep tea with cloves and cool. Combine juices with tea mixture and add ginger ale and rum. Serve in ice filled glasses and garnish with mint and fruit slices.

TEA SANDWICHES AND TIDBITS

TEA SANDWICH IDEAS

Tea sandwiches should look as good as they taste. Use your prettiest trays and platters and be sure to garnish with fresh herbs, flowers and fruit. For variety, make some of your own quick breads and freeze them weeks ahead. Order others from your favorite bakery. Consider using egg, whole wheat, black bread, rye or cheddar breads. Sweet breads such as banana, date nut, zucchini, orange or lemon are also delightful. Breads should be thinly sliced and the crusts removed. Traditional circles, rolls, fingers, triangles and squares are quick to make. Consider using different cookie cutters to fit the occasion as well. Hearts and flowers are always fun.

Spread each slice with softened butter or mayonnaise. Leave some of the sandwiches open face. A certain uniformity and precision makes your presentation all the more special. Place the sandwiches on cookie sheets and cover them with a damp towel to keep them from drying out. Cover tightly with plastic wrap and store in the refrigerator.

Here are some ideas to get you started:
- whole wheat bread, herbed cream cheese and English cucumbers

- Brie cheese, ham and green peppercorn mustard on black bread
- rye bread, unsalted butter, avocado, sliced hard cooked egg and a dollop of black caviar
- mozzarella cheese, sliced plum tomato and a sprig of fresh basil on tiny baguettes
- radish butter on whole wheat garnished with watercress
- dilled cream cheese, thinly sliced cucumber and baby shrimp on white bread
- smoked salmon, cream cheese and sliced scallion on wheat bread
- mascarpone cheese on black bread
- ground ham, green peppercorns, Dijon mustard and mayonnaise on cheddar bread
- cream cheese, chutney, curry and toasted almonds on banana bread
- deviled egg and chives on egg bread
- smoked turkey, mayonnaise and roasted red pepper on rye bread
- pineapple cream cheese on mango bread

PUMPKIN TEA SANDWICHES

3 loaves

This bread is tasty spread with orange butter or cream cheese combined with mango chutney. It's also delicious with curried chicken topped with toasted almonds. This bread freezes well and also makes a nice gift.

9 oz. butter
2 tbs. molasses
3 cups sugar
6 eggs
1 cup orange juice
1 can (30 oz.) pumpkin
5 cups flour

1 tsp. baking powder
1 tbs. baking soda
1 tsp. salt
1½ tsp. cinnamon
1½ tsp. cloves
1½ cups currants

In an electric mixer, cream butter, molasses and sugar until light. Add eggs, and beat until lemon colored. Add orange juice and pumpkin and combine well. Sift together the dry ingredients and add to batter, mix well. Stir in currants.

Prepare three 9-inch loaf pans by greasing well and lining with parchment. Butter the parchment. Divide batter evenly among pans and bake in a preheated 350° oven for 1 hour, or until a toothpick inserted in the center comes out clean. Cool in pans for 10 minutes. Turn out onto racks to cool.

ORANGE BUTTER

½ cup butter
¼ cup orange marmalade

Combine and chill.

MANGO SPREAD

8 oz. cream cheese, softened
½ cup mango chutney

Combine and chill.

WATERCRESS TEA SANDWICHES

32 small sandwiches

The ultimate in tea sandwiches, these were featured at the Savoy Hotel in London at their afternoon tea.

½ cup butter, softened
½ cup finely chopped watercress sprigs
2 tsp. grated onion
¾ tsp. Worcestershire sauce
¼ tsp. salt
¼ tsp. white pepper
watercress sprigs for garnish
1 loaf (16 oz.) thinly sliced white bread

Combine butter, watercress sprigs and seasonings. Roll bread slices flat with a rolling pin and spread with butter mixture. Roll up. Cover with a damp paper towel, which has been wrung out tightly, and wrap well with plastic wrap. Refrigerate for up to 24 hours. Before serving, bring to room temperature, cut each sandwich in half and insert sprigs of watercress into each end.

ASPARAGUS ROLL-UPS

75 sandwiches

These dainty tea savories are a bit time-consuming to make, but they freeze beautifully and have a wonderful flavor. Make them at your leisure and wait for the compliments!

25 slices white bread
25 blanched fresh asparagus spears
8 oz. cream cheese, room
  temperature

3 oz. blue cheese, crumbled
1 egg
white pepper to taste
1½ cups butter, melted

Blanch asparagus in boiling water or microwave and cool completely. Blot dry. Remove crusts from white bread and flatten with a rolling pin. Combine cream cheese, blue cheese and egg until smooth. Season to taste with white pepper. Spread evenly over bread slices. Place an asparagus spear on one side of each slice. Trim stem if necessary. Roll up tightly. Melt butter in a shallow pan. Dip rolls in butter and place on a cookie sheet. Cover well and freeze until use.

To serve: Preheat oven to 400°. Cut frozen rolls into thirds and bake while frozen, for 15 minutes or until golden. Serve hot.

SPECIAL CHICKEN FILLING

3 cups

The crunch of toasted hazelnuts, the sweetness of dates and the touch of bacon make this filling perfect for your most discriminating guests. Toast hazelnuts for 12 minutes at 350°, cool and rub between towels to remove their skins before chopping.

2 whole chicken breasts, poached and diced
1 cup finely chopped pitted dates
½ cup chopped toasted hazelnuts
½ cup crumbled crisp bacon
1 cup mayonnaise
salt to taste

Combine all ingredients and chill. Spread on buttered bread (white or wheat) and remove crusts. Cut into triangles for serving.

JOANNA'S DATE BREAD

1 loaf

Moist and delicious, this is so good spread with pineapple cream cheese. It's nice to garnish these with a tiny wedge of fresh strawberry and a sprig of mint.

1/4 cup butter
2 cups boiling water
1 pound pitted dates
2 tsp. baking soda
2 cups sugar
3½ cups flour
1 cup coarsely chopped walnuts

Bring water to a boil in a saucepan. Add butter and dates and let cool. When cool, add remaining ingredients in order listed. Preheat oven to 325°. Grease a bread pan and line the bottom with a piece of parchment or brown paper. Pour batter into pan and bake for 1 hour or until loaf tests done. Wrap well and refrigerate or freeze.

MANGO BREAD

2 loaves

If fresh mangoes are not available, use frozen mango juice concentrate or canned mangoes well drained.

¾ cup oil
2 eggs
1¼ cups sugar
2 cups flour
2 tsp. soda
2 tsp. cinnamon

½ tsp. salt
1 tsp. lemon juice
2½ cups chopped mangoes
1 cup raisins
1 cup coarsely chopped walnuts

In an electric mixer, combine oil, egg and sugar. Sift together flour, soda, cinnamon and salt. Add to egg mixture. Stir in lemon juice, mangoes, raisins and nuts. Pour into 2 greased 8x4-inch bread pans.

Preheat oven to 350°. Bake for 1 hours, or until center of loaves test done. Cool. Wrap in foil and refrigerate or freeze. Excellent spread with pineapple cream cheese.

STRAWBERRY TEA BREAD

2 loaves

A moist bread which is delicious spread with strawberry or honey butter.

2 cups sugar
4 eggs
1¼ cups melted butter
2 pkg. (10 oz. each) frozen strawberries, including juice, thawed
3 cups flour
1 tsp. baking powder
1 tsp. salt
3 tsp. cinnamon
1¼ cups chopped pecans

Preheat oven to 350° Grease and flour 2 bread pans. Using an electric mixer, beat sugar, eggs and melted butter. Add strawberries including juice. Sift together flour, baking powder, salt and cinnamon. Add to strawberry mixture. Stir in pecans. Pour batter into pans. Bake for 1 hour. Cool for 10 minutes in the pan and then turn out onto wire racks.

CREAM SCONES

For best results, make sure your baking powder is fresh.

1¾ cup flour
2 tsp. baking powder
1 tbs. sugar
½ tsp. salt

¼ cup butter
2 eggs, beaten
⅓ cup cream
1 tbs. sugar

Sift flour, baking powder, sugar and salt into a bowl. Cut butter into flour mixture using a pastry blender. Mixture should look like small peas. In another bowl, beat eggs and reserve 2 tbs. for glaze. Beat all but 2 tbs. of the eggs with cream. Add to flour mixture using swift strokes.

Divide dough in half. Pat each half out on a lightly floured board forming a circle ¾-inch thick, which is higher in the center. Cut each piece into 6 pie-shaped wedges. Place on a greased baking sheet with the thicker points facing the center of the sheet. Brush with the reserved beaten egg and sprinkle with the sugar.

Bake at 450° for 15 minutes, or until light gold. Serve hot with an assortment of jams.

SESAME CHEESE STRAWS

4 dozen

There are cheese straws and there are cheese straws - these are THE BEST!

2 cups flour
2/3 cup butter
2 cups sharp shredded cheddar cheese
1/2 cup toasted sesame seeds
1 tsp. salt
1 tsp. ground ginger
1 tsp. Worcestershire sauce
4 to 5 tbs. cold water

Preheat oven to 400°. In a food processor using the steel blade, combine flour and butter. Add cheese and seasonings until mixture resembles coarse crumbs. Sprinkle with cold water and process until mixture begins to form a ball. Remove dough from the machine and roll out as for pie crust on a lightly floured board. Cut into decorative strips using a pastry cutter or sharp knife. Place on a lightly greased baking sheet and bake for 10 to 12 minutes or until golden. Cool on a wire rack. Store in air tight containers. These freeze well.

CHEESE AND DATE PASTRIES

4 dozen

These are one of our all-time favorite snacks. The combination of tangy cheese, hot pepper, sweet dates and crunchy walnuts is hard to resist.

1 cup butter
8 oz. sharp cheddar cheese, shredded
2 cups flour

1 pound pitted dates
1 cup walnuts
salt and cayenne pepper to taste

Using the steel blade of a food processor, combine butter, cheese and flour until well blended. Add dates, walnuts and seasoning; process briefly to chop dates and nuts into mixture. Remove dough from workbowl and form into long rolls, about 2 inches in diameter. Wrap well in plastic wrap or foil and chill until firm. May be refrigerated or frozen at this point.

To bake, preheat oven to 300°. Slice dough into ¼-inch slices and place on lightly greased cookie sheets. Bake for 20 to 30 minutes or until edges are just beginning to brown. Remove from cookie sheets and cool on wire racks. May be served hot or at room temperature. Store in an air-tight container.

SALMON-STUFFED CHERRY TOMATOES

3 dozen

These cheery little morsels always disappear from a tea tray in a hurry. This mixture is also good piped onto English cucumber rounds.

3 dozen cherry tomatoes
8 oz. cream cheese, softened
4 oz. butter, softened

4 oz. smoked salmon, chopped
4 green onions, sliced
sprigs of parsley

Hollow out cherry tomatoes using a grapefruit spoon. Turn upside down to drain on paper towels.

Using the steel knife of a food processor or an electric mixer, combine cream cheese and butter until light. Stir in remaining ingredients. Spoon or pipe into cherry tomatoes, garnish with a small leaf of parsley and refrigerate until serving.

Variations:

- Fill tomatoes with guacamole.
- Use baby shrimp, crab meat or crumbled bacon instead of smoked salmon.

STUFFED STRAWBERRIES

3 dozen

For a tea party, it's always charming to include a selection of fresh fruit. I like to use grape clusters, slices of kiwi, starfruit and these pretty berries. They look so professional and are easy to do ahead. A pastry bag is essential.

2 to 3 dozen pretty strawberries
8 oz. cream cheese, softened
½ cup powdered sugar
1 tbs. Grand Marnier or orange juice
grated zest of 1 orange

Remove green tops from strawberries. Cut pointed end into wedges like a pie, cutting about ⅔ of the way down. If the berry is small, make two cuts; if large, make three cuts, dividing the berry into 6 wedges.

Combine cream cheese, sugar, Grand Marnier and zest using a food processor or mixer until well blended. Place in a pastry bag fitted with a fluted tip. Pipe mixture into center of each berry. Garnish with mint leaves or flower if desired. Can be stored in the refrigerator for several hours.

GOOD WITH TEA: MUFFINS, COOKIES, TARTS AND PUDDINGS

ORANGE MUFFINS

These muffins have a delicious citrus flavor that is a perfect accompaniment to a refreshing cup of tea.

½ cup orange juice
¼ cup vegetable oil
1 cup butter
1 cup sugar
4 eggs, separated

½ cup orange marmalade
2 tsp. grated orange zest
2½ cups flour
2 tsp. baking powder
1 tsp. salt

Preheat oven to 375°. Grease 24 two-inch muffin cups. Combine orange juice and oil in a 1-cup glass measure. Beat butter with sugar and egg yolks until light and fluffy. Add marmalade and orange zest. Sift together flour, baking powder and salt. Add alternately to butter-egg mixture with orange juice and oil. In a separate bowl, beat egg whites until stiff. Fold into batter. Spoon evenly into prepared muffin cups. Bake 20 minutes or until golden.

APRICOT BARS

These are a snap to make and taste great.

1 cup butter
1 cup sugar
1 egg yolk
2 cups flour
¾ cup walnuts
1 jar (10 oz.) apricot jam

Preheat oven to 350°. Grease a 9x13-inch baking pan. In a food processor using the steel blade, combine butter, sugar, egg, flour and nuts until crumbly. Pat half of the mixture on the bottom of prepared pan. Spread with jam and crumble remaining dough on top. Bake for 40 to 45 minutes. Cool and cut into bars.

MARMALADE COOKIES

3 dozen

These cookies are perfect with a cup of Constant Comment tea.

½ cup butter
1 cup sugar
2 eggs, beaten
3 cups flour

½ tsp. soda
½ tsp. salt
1 cup orange marmalade

Using an electric mixer, cream butter, sugar and eggs until light. Add flour, soda and salt. Stir in marmalade. Drop by rounded teaspoons 1 inch apart on greased cookie sheets. Bake at 350° for 10 to 12 minutes. Cool on wire racks.

FROSTING

¼ cup orange juice
2 tsp. orange zest
1 tsp. lemon juice

1 tsp. lemon zest
3 tbs. butter
3 cups powdered sugar

Combine frosting ingredients in a food processor using the steel knife. Frost cooled cookies.

BUTTER PECAN BARS

2 dozen

This decadent recipe is like blond brownies with pecan pie filling on top.

¾ cup butter
1½ cups brown sugar
2 eggs

2 tsps. vanilla
1¾ cups flour
1 tsp. soda

Using the steel knife of a food processor or an electric mixer, mix butter, sugar, egg and vanilla until creamy. Add flour and soda. Preheat oven to 350°. Grease and flour a 9x13-inch pan. Spread batter in pan, smoothing evenly. Bake for 15 minutes.

TOPPING

½ cup butter
½ cup honey
½ cup brown sugar

1 tsp. instant coffee
3 tbs. cream
3 cups pecans, chopped

In a heavy saucepan, melt butter. Stir in honey, brown sugar, coffee and cream. Over medium heat, bring to a boil stirring constantly. Remove from heat. Add pecans and pour onto prepared crust. Bake at 350° for 25 minutes. Cool and cut into bars.

HONEY NUT CHEWS

2 dozen

To enhance the appearance of these cookies, drizzle thin lines of melted white and dark chocolate diagonally across the top. Pretty!

CRUST

⅔ cups powdered sugar
2 cups flour

1 cup butter

Preheat oven to 350°. Grease and flour a 9x13-inch baking pan. Using the steel blade of a food processor, or an electric mixer, combine crust ingredients until crumbly and pat into prepared pan. Bake for 20 minutes and cool.

TOPPING

1 cup slivered almonds
1 cup coarsely chopped walnuts
1 cup coarsely chopped pecans

½ cup butter, melted
½ cup honey
½ cup brown sugar

Prepare nuts by rinsing them in a strainer. Spread on a cookie sheet and bake at 350° for 5 to 10 minutes, until completely dry and lightly toasted. In a large bowl, stir together melted butter, honey and brown sugar. Add toasted nuts and stir to coat well. Spread carefully over prepared crust and bake at 350° for 20 to 25 minutes. Cool and drizzle with melted chocolate, if desired. Cut into bars.

PECAN TASSIES

4 dozen

Teflon-lined miniature muffin tins are also good for appetizers and desserts.

CRUST

1 cup butter
6 oz. cream cheese

2 cups flour

Preheat oven to 350°. Using the steel blade of a food processor, combine butter, cream cheese and flour until it forms a smooth dough. Remove from workbowl and divide evenly into fourths. Divide each portion into 12 small balls. Spray 4 miniature muffin pans (12 muffins each) with nonstick coating. Press each ball of dough into a muffin cup evenly on bottom and up sides to rim.

FILLING

½ cup butter, softened
1 cup sugar
2 eggs, beaten

1½ cup pecans, chopped
1 cup dates, pitted and chopped
2 tsp. vanilla

Cream together butter and eggs. Stir in remaining ingredients. Divide evenly among unbaked shells. Fill completely. Bake until golden brown, about 30 to 40 minutes. Cool before removing from tins. If desired, sprinkle with powdered sugar before serving.

CHERRY SQUARES

2 dozen

This is one of my favorite cookie recipes, perfect for a tea party.

CRUST
½ cup butter
1 tbs. powdered sugar

1 cup flour

Mix together and press into a greased 9x13-inch baking pan. Bake at 300° for 25 minutes.

FILLING
2 eggs
1 cup brown sugar
8 oz. maraschino cherries, chopped
2 tbs. flour
½ tsp. baking powder

¼ cup chopped pitted dates
½ cup flaked coconut
½ cup chopped walnuts
½ tsp. almond extract

Combine filling ingredients until well mixed and pour over baked base. Bake at 350° for 30 minutes. Frost while hot.

FROSTING

4 oz. cream cheese
2 tbs. butter
½ tsp. almond extract
1½ to 2 cups powdered sugar

Combine frosting ingredients and spread on cookies while still warm. Cool and cut into bars.

ALMOND TART

This delicious tart is so versatile! In the winter top it with pears and cranberries, in the spring strawberries and kiwi, and in summer apricots and blueberries or peaches and raspberries.

PASTRY

12 tbs. butter

1/2 cup powdered sugar

1¼ cups flour

Combine ingredients using the steel blade of a food processor. Press in the bottom and up the sides of an 11-inch tart pan. Prick bottom with a fork. Bake at 350° for 20 minutes. Cool.

FILLING

4 oz. almond paste

8 oz. cream cheese, cubed

1/4 cup sugar

1 egg

1/2 tsp. vanilla

1/2 tsp. almond extract

Combine all ingredients until smooth, using the steel blade of a food processor. Pour into prepared crust. Bake at 375° for 10 minutes, cool and top with fruits of your choice as suggested below.

Pears and cranberries: Drain 6 canned pear halves and blot dry with paper towels. Arrange on top of tart with rounded side up and narrow ends pointed towards center. Heat 1 can whole berry cranberry sauce until melted. Stir in 1 tbs. orange juice, marmalade or Grand Marnier. Spoon cranberries around pears and brush tops of pears with some of the sauce. Refrigerate until serving.

Strawberries and kiwi: Stem and halve 1 basket fresh strawberries. Peel and slice 2 kiwi fruit. Arrange decoratively on top of tart. Heat ½ cup apricot jam with 1 tbs. brandy and brush on fruit as a glaze. Refrigerate.

Apricot and blueberry: Use drained canned apricot halves or poached fresh ones. Place rounded side up on top of tart and place fresh large blueberries in between. Brush with apricot glaze, as above. Refrigerate.

Peach and raspberry: Peel and slice fresh peaches. Arrange in a ying/yang fashion on top of tart, using peaches for one side and fresh raspberries for the other. Brush with apricot glaze and refrigerate.

RASPBERRY KUCHEN

16 to 20 wedges

This is a buttery rich Dutch cookie, perfect to serve with tea. Its success depends on using a quality jam — we like raspberry or apricot. And NEVER use anything but real butter!!

2⅔ cups flour
1⅓ cups sugar
1⅓ cups butter
½ tsp. salt
1 egg
2 cups jam, raspberry or apricot

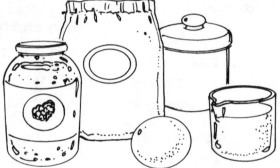

Using the steel blade of a food processor, combine flour, sugar, butter and salt until crumbly. Press ⅔ of the dough on the bottom of a buttered 9-inch springform pan. Spread with jam. Crumble remaining dough on top. Bake at 350° for 45 minutes or until golden. Cool and cut into small wedges to serve.

AMARETTO BREAD PUDDING

Servings: 8 to 12

Try this with a cup of apricot tea. A bain marie is a French water bath. Set baking dish into a larger pan and pour boiling water half way up the side of the dish.

1½ lbs. egg bread, torn into pieces
4½ cups milk
1½ cups cream
5 eggs, beaten
2¼ cups sugar

3 tbs. almond extract
1 cup dried apricots, chopped
2 cups golden raisins
1¼ cups slivered almonds

Pour milk and cream over bread and let stand for 10 minutes. Combine remaining ingredients and mix well with softened bread. Pour into a well-buttered baking dish and bake at 350° for 50 to 60 minutes in a *bain marie*.

AMARETTO SAUCE

1 cup butter
2 cups powdered sugar, sifted

2 eggs, beaten
½ cup amaretto

Melt butter in a saucepan over low heat. Stir in powdered sugar and eggs, whisking constantly. Add amaretto to taste. Pour hot sauce over individual servings of the bread pudding.

RAISIN BREAD PUDDING

Servings: 10 to 12

This is comfort food at its best. Add a cup of hot tea and you're all set!

1 loaf (16 oz.) cinnamon raisin bread
1 quart milk
3 eggs

2 cups sugar
2 tbs. vanilla
1 tbs. butter

Tear bread into large pieces and place in a large mixing bowl. Pour milk over and stir to coat. Let bread soak 15 minutes.

Beat eggs, sugar and vanilla until thick and smooth. Pour over bread mixture and combine well. Place in a well buttered baking dish. Preheat oven to 350°. Place pudding in a larger pan and fill with 2 inches of hot water. Bake for 1 hour, or until set. If desired, serve with *Whiskey Sauce*.

WHISKEY SAUCE

1 cup heavy cream
4 egg yolks

1 cup powdered sugar
¼ cup whiskey

Beat cream until stiff. Beat egg yolks in a separate bowl; add powdered sugar and whip until light. Add whiskey and fold in whipped cream.

INDEX

SERVE CREATIVE, EASY, NUTRITIOUS MEALS WITH NITTY GRITTY® COOKBOOKS

The Versatile Rice Cooker
The Dehydrator Cookbook
Waffles
The Coffee Book
The Bread Machine Cookbook
The Bread Machine Cookbook II
The Bread Machine Cookbook III
The Bread Machine Cookbook IV
The Sandwich Maker Cookbook
The Juicer Book
The Juicer Book II
Bread Baking (traditional), revised
The Kid's Cookbook, revised
The Kid's Microwave Cookbook
15-Minute Meals for 1 or 2
Recipes for the 9x13 Pan
Turkey, the Magic Ingredient

Chocolate Cherry Tortes and Other Lowfat Delights
Lowfat American Favorites
Lowfat International Cuisine
The Hunk Cookbook
Now That's Italian!
Fabulous Fiber Cookery
Low Salt, Low Sugar, Low Fat Desserts
What's for Breakfast?
Healthy Cooking on the Run
Healthy Snacks for Kids
Creative Soups & Salads
Quick & Easy Pasta Recipes, revised
Muffins, Nut Breads and More
The Barbecue Book
The Wok

New Ways with Your Wok
Quiche & Soufflé Cookbook
Easy Microwave Cooking
Cooking for 1 or 2
Meals in Minutes
New Ways to Enjoy Chicken
Favorite Seafood Recipes
No Salt, No Sugar, No Fat Cookbook
New International Fondue Cookbook
Extra-Special Crockery Pot Recipes
Favorite Cookie Recipes
Authentic Mexican Cooking
Fisherman's Wharf Cookbook
The Creative Lunch Box

Write or call for our free catalog.
Bristol Publishing Enterprises, Inc.
P.O. Box 1737, San Leandro, CA 94577
(800)346-4889; in California (510)895-4461